WHEN PARENTS HAVE PROBLEMS

The Runaway

Once when the snow of the year was beginning to fall,
  We stopped by a mountain pasture to say, "Whose colt?"
A little Morgan had one forefoot on the wall,
The other curled at his breast. He dipped his head
And snorted at us. And then he had to bolt.
We heard the miniature thunder where he fled,
And we saw him, or thought we saw him, dim and grey,
Like a shadow against the curtain of falling flakes.
"I think the little fellow's afraid of the snow.
He isn't winter-broken. It isn't play
With the little fellow at all. He's running away.
I doubt if even his mother could tell him, 'Sakes,
It's only weather.' He'd think she didn't know
Where is his mother? He can't be out alone!"
And now he comes again with the clatter of stone
And mounts the wall again with whited eyes
And all his tail that isn't hair up straight.
He shudders his coat as if to throw off flies.
"Whoever it is that leaves him out so late,
When other creatures have gone to stall and bin,
Ought to be told to come and take him in."

ROBERT FROST

Second Edition

WHEN PARENTS HAVE PROBLEMS

A Book for Teens and Older Children
Who Have a Disturbed or Difficult Parent

By

SUSAN B. MILLER, Ph.D.

CHARLES C THOMAS • PUBLISHER, LTD.
Springfield • Illinois • U.S.A.

Published and Distributed Throughout the World by

CHARLES C THOMAS • PUBLISHER, LTD.
2600 South First Street
Springfield, Illinois 62704

© 2012 by CHARLES C THOMAS • PUBLISHER, LTD.

ISBN 978-0-398-08713-5 (paper)
ISBN 978-0-398-08714-2 (ebook)

First Edition, 1995
Second Edition, 2012

Library of Congress Catalog Card Number: 2011036336

With THOMAS BOOKS *careful attention is given to all details of manufacturing
and design. It is the Publisher's desire to present books that are satisfactory as to their
physical qualities and artistic possibilities and appropriate for their particular use.*
THOMAS BOOKS *will be true to those laws of quality that assure a good name
and good will.*

*Printed in the United States of America
MM-R-3*

Library of Congress Cataloging-in-Publication Data

Miller, Susan B. (Susan Beth)
    When parents have problems : a book for teens and older children
who have a disturbed or difficult parent / by Susan B. Miller. -- 2nd ed.
        p. cm.
    ISBN 978-0-398-08713-5 (pbk.) -- ISBN 978-0-398-08714-2 (ebook)
    1. Abused children--United States--Juvenile literature. 2. Abusive par-
ents--United States--Psychology--Juvenile literature. 3. Psychological
child abuse--United States--Juvenile literature. 4. Parents--Mental
health--Juvenile literature. 5. Self-help techniques--United States--
Juvenile literature. I. Title.

    HV6626.52 M543 2012
    362.76'30973--dc23
                                                    2011036336

In memory of my aunt, Rose M. Wovell

ABOUT THE AUTHOR

Susan B. Miller is a clinical psychologist in private practice in Ann Arbor, Michigan. She works with young people and adults in psychotherapy and also spends time writing fiction and non-fiction. She is the author of a novel, *Indigo Rose* (Bantam Dell, 2004) and three books on psychology: *The Shame Experience* (The Analytic Press, 1985), *Shame in Context* (The Analytic Press, 1996) and *Disgust: The Gatekeeper Emotion* (The Analytic Press, 2004). Favorite pastimes include natural areas stewardship and time spent with kids and animals.

PREFACE

In writing the second edition of this book, I have made changes through-out in order to update and to refine my ideas. I have also added two chapters. The first addresses parents who have difficult personalities. These parents are not openly abusive or obviously neglectful to their kids, but they present them with many challenges. In this new chapter, I talk about over-protective parents, parents who are perfectionists, and immature parents. Other examples of parents with difficult personalities could have been given. Some readers will supply their own. The second new chapter addresses parents in poverty. Some families are poor by any standard, and some are poor in relation to their community. Either type of poverty is difficult for a child. The problems of poverty may be different for a teenager than for a younger child. I look at a range of challenges associated with poverty.

Many books have been written for adults who grew up coping with trou-bled parents. Often the adults who read these books say, "I wish someone had told me that when I was a kid. It might have helped me so much." Unfortunately, not much has been written for the kids who are coping *in the present* with difficult or troubled parents. In part, that's because kids may be hesitant to read books about tough subjects, so publishers hesitate to invest money in publishing them. It's also because kids sometimes get their books from parents and troubled parents seldom recognize their own problems or encourage their kids to read books about living with those problems.

It's also true that kids with troubled parents sometimes feel funny about recognizing their parents' shortcomings. They may feel even more uncom-fortable about bringing home a book that talks about troubled mothers and fathers, or keeping a book like that in a school locker. Some kids or teens would feel guilty or disloyal reading such a book, even though it's a smart, sensible thing to do and it isn't something that will hurt their parents. So there are lots of reasons few books have been written for young people who have parents who are ill, are alcoholic, are abusive, or are troubled in some other way.

There are also some very good reasons to write such a book and to en-courage young people to read it. Difficult childhoods often lead to unnecessary pain and struggle later in life. This book is written with the idea that intelligent kids can use sound ideas to improve their lives, either on their own or with the help of healthy adults. In this book, I try to offer help in sorting out whether a difficult situation may be a result of a parent's problems.

The idea isn't to belittle or undermine your parents or to blame them for things that are your responsibility. The idea is to be realistic about the sources of a problem and, if a parent's difficulties is one of those sources, to help you deal better with your situation. I try to give you an idea of the kinds of problems or challenges your parent's troubles can cause for you. I also give you ideas on how to deal constructively with your parent's problems so that you can keep on track with your own growing up.

You may agree with some of my ideas and disagree with others. Some you'll find useful and others may not be of value to you or relevant to your situation. But I hope reading the book and considering the ideas will help you take some steps along a road worth traveling.

S.B.M.

ACKNOWLEDGMENTS

Many people were helpful to me during the writing of this book. I would especially like to thank my father for the support he has given me for my writing, over many years, even when little success was coming my way. My thanks also to my sisters, Lisa Sablosky and Laura Eligator, who are my constants. My aunt, Rose M. Wovell, has died since the publication of the first edition. She was a special source of love and wisdom, and a person of courage to whom this book is dedicated. I am also grateful for the support and editorial help of friends during the writing of the second edition of this book. Those friends include but are not limited to Judy Gray, Julia Davies, Nancy and Irv Leon, Lois Dowling, Rose Diliscia-Everett, and Judith Saltzman.

The idea for this book came from my work with a bright young woman who was finding it hard to make sense of her life with a troubled parent. As I began to think about writing this book, many other young and older people came into my thoughts, all of whom had told me their stories of growing up. My thanks to them for sharing portions of their lives with me. Finally, my thanks to Charles C Thomas Publisher, for their willingness to publish this book on a difficult topic and their responsiveness throughout the process.

CONTENTS

WHEN PARENTS HAVE PROBLEMS

Chapter 1

GETTING STARTED

I've written this book for kids whose parents have problems. Of course, all parents at times have problems, but some parents have problems that are serious and lasting, which makes them poor parents a lot of the time. This book is especially for kids whose parents have major, lasting problems. If you are one of these kids–whether a younger child, a teenager, or even a young adult–you have special challenges in growing up since your parents often are unable to help you; sometimes they stand smack in your way. I've tried to write this book in plain language so it will be within reach of kids not older than ten or eleven, but the ideas presented hold true for people of all ages.

Troubled parents are not all the same. Some parents are abusive or neglectful; their kids may find them cruel or uncaring. Some parents suffer a great deal because of a mental illness or a painful loss or a difficult set of experiences they've not been able to overcome; their children may pity them and feel helpless about their suffering. Other parents have dangerous habits such as drug or alcohol abuse, shoplifting or gambling; or they do distressing things such as carrying on extramarital affairs. You wish they'd stop what they're doing, but they don't, no matter how much they hurt the people around them. Though troubled parents come in many forms, they present some shared challenges and difficulties for their children.

You may be wondering why you should read a book like this. Thinking about parents' problems isn't pleasant. Many kids work hard to believe their parents have no serious problems, even when the evidence points in the other direction. You may love your parents very much, or want to love them, and feel it's not right to think of them as troubled. But, unless you're an ostrich, it's best not to stick your head in the sand. Seeing what's true—even if that truth isn't pretty—helps you to cope better with the real situation you're in. Seeing an unpleasant truth is never a reason to feel guilty. Recognizing what's there doesn't make you disloyal or unkind; it doesn't mean you're trying to hurt or shame your parent. You're not creating the problem; you're just seeing it, which is better than closing your eyes and your mind.

Another approach kids may take to their parents' problems is to try to live as if their parents mean nothing at all to them and as if they need no parents. That's an understandable strategy if your parent causes you pain and difficulty, but it has its limitations. All kids need parenting. Nature made us that way. We grow up gradually, over many years, and we need a great deal of help along the way.

Depending on the particular parent you have, some parts of this book may be more meaningful to you than others. For example, if you have an overanxious parent who is generally kind and attentive, the part of the book about mistreatment may not speak to you as much as other parts will. If you have an abusive parent who terrorizes you or your brothers or sisters, the parts of the book about feeling sad about your parent's suffering may not be what you need, since you may feel much more angry than sad. On the other hand, some kids with abusive parents do feel sad for their parents, and also angry. If some of the sections don't seem to apply to you, you can skip them or you may want to read them anyway. Maybe they'll help you better understand a friend.

You might wonder why I got interested in writing this book. One reason is that I am a psychologist and my work has given me many opportunities to see how often kids with troubled parents can make good use of a little advice and a little support. I'd like to offer those things to more kids through this book. A second reason is that I myself was one of the many kids who grew up having to cope with a troubled parent. I know how confusing it can be and how much a young person can use some help sorting things out. Kids with troubled parents have strengths they can use to cope with their situation. I'm hoping this book can help you make fuller use of your strengths.

I want to say a bit more about the particular kinds of problems parents can have. Sometimes a parent's problems show up most clearly as behaviors a child wishes the parent would stop, but the parent doesn't stop. For example, your mother drinks too much and gets nasty or sexually inappropriate when she's drinking. Or your father gambles and wastes the family's money so there's not enough for rent, school expenses or good food. Or maybe your father or mother has affairs, making for lots of tension between the two adults on whom you rely. Often they seem to hate each other and you may wish (but fear) that they would just divorce. Or your mother uses drugs and may be spaced-out or doing irresponsible, frightening things like feeding your baby sister food that's not good for her or driving recklessly; maybe she gets arrested or she makes you angry by lying in bed all day.

Parents' problems can come in other forms as well. Some parents are always unhappy and they complain to their children about how miserable they are. Kids worry that their mother or father might go on feeling sad forever or might commit suicide. Some parents feel very anxious and jittery, or they can't go out of the house without getting panicky. And some parents have a mental illness so they can't function at all normally; they have odd experiences, like hallucinations, that their kids don't understand; or they talk a mile a minute about crazy-sounding things and stay up all night; or they're convinced against all reason that the neighbors are trying to poison them. A mentally ill parent may have too much on his mind or too much wrong with his mind to take care of you. He may neglect you entirely, or confuse your needs with his own or your brother's, or he may attend to you but give you bad advice that's due to his mixed-up thinking. For example, a paranoid parent may tell you to wear a disguise if you have to go to the neighbor's to borrow the lawn mower, or to watch out for the woman that lives in the green house because she's trying to kill your family or to listen in on your thoughts. Or a manic parent may insist you go out shopping with him at four in the morning. Or he might want to spend hours showing you sexy pictures on the Internet and think that's incredibly funny and fun but then snap at you if you're not amused.

Some troubled parents have no obvious illness, but yet something is something wrong with them. They may get along poorly with other adults. Maybe your mother gets into arguments and is rude to people so that you feel nervous and embarrassed when you're out in public with her. She may blow up at a waitress over some tiny thing or insult your schoolteacher. Some parents show their problems by being over-critical of others. They may get down on everyone around them; or they may pick one child or adult on whom to harp, for no good reason; they may pick one person to fault today, and someone else tomorrow. Other troubled parents may be overprotective and overanxious, or they may be huge perfectionists who are unable to relax or let you relax. They're nice enough but you don't feel very good around them.

You may feel confused about whether the problems you experience at home are yours or your parent's. That distinction can be hard to make, especially because both you and your parent may be making a contribution. Nevertheless, it can be valuable to try to sort it out, especially if you are the kind of person who tends to take blame for everything that goes wrong.

Let me give you a few guidelines that can help you get a better perspective on whether you have a troubled parent. These guidelines focus less on extreme behaviors (such as drug abuse or physical mistreatment) than on how your parent feels about you and acts toward you. They concern the relationship between you and your parent. I'll start with the idea that all people, whatever their age, have their own unique feelings and thoughts and their own needs and wishes. Each person has the right to expect that his feelings, thoughts, needs, and wishes will be treated with respect and taken into consideration by the people around him, especially by the adults who are there to care for him. Having your feelings and needs respected and considered does not mean that you'll always get what you want or that your needs will be put above everyone else's. It does mean that your parents will have an interest in knowing what your feelings and needs are and that they will not ignore or ridicule them.

One clear sign that a parent has serious problems is when the parent cannot look at the needs and wishes, feelings and thoughts of his or her child. The "not looking" may take a variety of forms. The parent may be too preoccupied with himself or caught up in the symptoms of his mental illness or addiction to notice or care. Or she may resent that her child's needs and feelings are different from her own so she ridicules the child. Or he may pay close attention to the child but come up with a very distorted view of the child's inner self, so that the child does not even recognize herself in the picture her parent paints. Or a parent may be attentive to the child some of the time but then become completely inattentive, perhaps because she is drinking too much, traveling all the time, going through a depression, or because she only pays attention to her child when he's doing something that meets her needs. Let me give an example of a troubled parent who is attentive to her child but paints a distorted picture of him that disregards his real feelings and needs:

> George is thirteen. His two best friends are going to summer camp for three weeks. George tells his mother he'd like to go to camp too. His mother's response is, "Wouldn't you be scared, George? You've never been away from home before." George says he's scared, but he wants to go. His friends are going and they're excited about it. He feels excited too, thinking of the fun he could have. His mother says she doesn't think George should go. He'll be too homesick and unhappy. He's not as adventurous as his friends and he's physically delicate. She tells him a story about her own bad experience at summer camp when she was thirteen. She details how lonely she was, how awful the food was and how the counselors were mean. George gets angry. "I'm not like you," he says. "I want to go to camp. I'm not delicate and I will have fun. You don't want me to have a good time," he yells. His mother gets furious. "Don't talk to me like that," she says. "I'm just trying to protect you. You've never been to camp before—I have. You've got a lot of nerve yelling at me when I'm looking out for your best interests. You talk big about camp now but wait till you get there and you're all alone." George feels confused, guilty, and dejected. And worse yet, he now feels very afraid to go to camp because he doesn't think his mom will support him.

George's mother is a troubled parent who appears to be looking at her child's feelings and needs, but actually she isn't. She probably believes she's being helpful to George, but she's only looking at George's fear, because it's like her own fear, and she's ignoring his wishes for adventure and friendship and his wishes to grow up and be on his own. She paints a picture of George that isn't accurate, then she tries to force it on him, and she gets angry and offended when he won't accept it. She pushes him to feel guilty for rejecting her "concern," and she takes no responsibility for discouraging George's excitement and his adventurous spirit.

A troubled parent often has difficulty looking at her child and seeing what is inside that child. She also has difficulty looking inside *herself* and noticing her own feelings and behaviors. This second difficulty means that the parent will have a hard time taking a *reasonable amount* of responsibility for how her parenting affects her child. I say a reasonable amount of responsibility because some parents take too little responsibility for their children's feelings, some take too much responsibility, and some are confused and take responsibility when they're not responsible but fail to take responsibility when they are.

All these difficulties cause confusion for the child or teen, who is trying to sort out how his own feelings and behaviors are related to his parent's behavior. A parent who takes too little responsibility doesn't recognize when her child's anger, sadness or stubbornness is a response to neglect or abuse from the parent. The parent blames the child for having upset feelings, as if the feelings are just an annoyance to the parent and aren't the child's legitimate response to the home he's living in. George's mother is an example. She gets angry at George for his complaints; she doesn't see that he has reason to complain about what she's done.

Parents who take too much responsibility also create problems for kids. If the child sneezes, the mom faults herself for not dressing the child properly. If the child gets a bad grade on a test he blew-off studying for, the dad feels responsible and gets depressed. Pretty soon the child feels trapped by his parent's excessive self-blaming. The child feels he has to be perfect (never get sick, never fail a test, and never feel sad) in order to protect the parent from worry. He may feel angry at his parent and then feel guilty for being angry at someone who worries so much about him. He may also get the feeling that nothing about him is his own, not even his problems. He has to share everything with his parent. He wants his own sneezes, his own bad grades, and of course his own good grades, too.

Some parents fault themselves at all the wrong times and leave their child confused about what reasonably can be expected from a parent. Such a parent may cruelly belittle a teenage son in public and not give that unkind behavior a thought, but then the parent apologizes to her son for not getting him an expensive computer for Christmas, when no apologies are needed. The child gets confused about his own importance. He feels very unimportant to his parent when that parent humiliates him without a thought; yet that same parent apologizes about not getting him a lavish gift, as if he were a prince who should have every single thing he wants and never a moment of frustration.

One more sign of a troubled parent is that the parent needs the child to be a certain way, even when that way of being is not natural to that child. The parent constantly pressures the child to change and cannot love the child as she is. A parent may need her child to be a certain way in order to make up for failings the parent sees in herself. A parent may need a child to be thin or stylish or very successful in school or very accomplished as an athlete or musician. The parent is seldom satisfied with the child as she is and the child feels unloved.

Parents may have other kinds of strong needs regarding what their children should be. Though this sounds odd, some parents need their children to be failures or to be unattractive or to be stupid. Maybe the parent feels stupid and she doesn't want to be alone with that bad feeling, so she expects her daughter to be stupid with her, to make the parent feel less deficient and alone. If the daughter does well in school, the mother might get irritable or ignore the child or she might fill the child's time with household responsibilities so she can't study and continue to do well in school. This kind of parent is so controlled by her own strong need for the child to be this way or that way that she's not able to look at what's natural and good for the child.

If you still feel uncertain whether your parent has a serious problem that's making for difficulty between the two of you, or making for difficulty in your own feelings, think about whether your parent pays attention to your thoughts and feelings, needs and wishes, and at least tries to get a pretty accurate view of those aspects of you. And think about whether your parent looks at his own behavior and how that behavior affects you. One last thing to look at is whether you can talk to your parent when you feel he's shortchanging you. Will he take an honest look at his own behavior if you ask him to? A healthy parent is willing to look at what he's doing and take responsibility when he's making mistakes. He won't fault himself for things you do or act as if you're a baby who's not responsible for his own actions. Neither will he blame you for everything and refuse to look at himself. He'll look honestly at himself and you both and do the best job he can figuring out who is doing what. The analysis he comes up with may not be exactly like your own, but it won't be totally different either. It will sound reasonable to you and you'll likely feel glad that you and your parent talked.

The remainder of this book considers different kinds of problems parents can have, how these problems can affect you, and how you can deal with them. Luckier kids have parents who don't have serious troubles that get in the way of their parenting. But even the happiest, healthiest parents sometimes do things that are unhelpful to their kids, and it's good for kids to know when that's happening.

Some of the kids reading this book are young women and some are young men. A few many be intersex. I'm going to go back and forth in addressing my comments to "she's" and "he's"; but keep in mind that I'm talking to everyone all the way through. The same goes for parents. Whether I'm referring to "he" or "she," the idea would hold true for any parent. I'm also trying to speak to people of differing ages, so I may refer at times to children, kids, or teens, and at times to young men or women.

Chapter 2

SELFISHNESS

To lay the groundwork for some ideas to come later, I want to talk a little about selfishness. Parents often criticize kids for selfishness. Sometimes, this kind of criticism makes sense and is helpful. Say you ask your younger sister to go to the park with you to shoot baskets, but when you get there one of your school friends is there by herself so you ditch your sister and go off to your friend's house. If your mom says you shouldn't have been so selfish, she has a point. In leaving your sister alone in the park, you were thinking *only* of your own wishes and you were neglecting your sister's wishes and welfare. That's what true selfishness is about: It's about thinking only of yourself and forgetting that others are people, too.

Unfortunately, some troubled parents fault their kids for selfishness when the criticism isn't deserved. Kids get called selfish when they're just trying to take good care of themselves by doing ordinary things such as making friends, studying, learning skills, enjoying jokes or interesting ideas, or feeling their own everyday feelings. They're not hurting or neglecting anyone else; they're just treating themselves with respect and valuing their own feelings and wishes.

Sometimes, unhelpful parents try to interfere with a young person's reasonable efforts to take good care of himself; they do that by saying he's selfish, meaning that he doesn't care about others. Some troubled parents use this selfishness-slam whenever a young person wants to do something that makes that child unavailable to take care of the parent's needs. Actually, it's the parent who is being selfish because she thinks her child should put all his own needs and wishes second to the parent's needs and wishes. Some very troubled parents think their kids shouldn't even have needs, wishes, and opinions of their own. If you have a parent who is troubled in that way, you will have to work hard not to get brainwashed. That is, you'll have to work hard to hold onto your own ideas and feelings and your right to have them.

Taking care of yourself is not selfish. Taking care of yourself is terrific. It's what you and I and everybody else is supposed to do. Our first job, which we were born to do, is taking care of our bodies, minds, and spirits. The better we do with that job, the more we'll be happy and comfortable and have an interest in helping out others. If we neglect ourselves and leave ourselves deprived and miserable, we won't be much use to others. That's obvious, right? But it's hard to hold onto if other people—especially those who are important to us—keep throwing this word "selfish" at us as if it's a horrible thing that makes them withhold their love and respect from us. Let's look at an example of a troubled parent faulting a child for selfishness.

Say you want quiet time to do your homework but your brother is racing around the house wrestling with three of his friends. You tell your mother you need quiet time to get your schoolwork done so that later on you can relax for a while and then get to bed at a reasonable hour. You ask if your brother and his friends could roughhouse outside. Rather than asking your brother to quiet down or go outside and play, your mother gets aggravated with you for making a request. She starts yelling that everybody wants something from her and she's exhausted and she might just pack up and leave and go somewhere where she's appreciated. She says you're selfish and never think about her needs. Since your mother's no help, you go yourself and ask your brother to play outside. He gets annoyed too, and raises his voice, and then your mother comes in and says, "Why do you have to start trouble? You're so selfish." Who's the selfish one in this story? Your mother sounds pretty selfish to me. She's the one who is only thinking about herself and isn't thinking about you and your reasonable wish for quiet. She's not thinking about her responsibilities as an adult and a parent, either, for example, her responsibility to help your brother learn to be considerate of others.

Here's another example. You've made plans two weeks in advance to go to the bead shop with your friend to buy supplies for earrings you and she are learning to make. Just before you're ready to go, your father decides he wants to play golf. He can't get a babysitter for your little sister, so he asks you to babysit. You tell him you've got plans with a friend and he tells you you're selfish and you never think of anyone but yourself. In this example and the one with the rowdy brothers, a parent uses the idea of selfishness as a weapon to hurt a child and as a manipulation to get the child to take over some of the parent's responsibilities. The parents in the examples are also trying to make the child feel like a bad person, even though the child is just taking care of his or her own needs, which are reasonable ones (the child isn't asking for a Ferrari or a trip to Tahiti or to have the little sister given away to the neighbors). If you can resist the kind of emotional blackmail shown in these examples, good for you. Even if you have no choice but to give up your visit to the bead shop or your quiet study time, try to keep clear in your own mind about what's selfish and what's not.

Now let's talk a little about unselfishness and what that means. Unselfishness doesn't mean neglecting yourself or letting yourself be mistreated just because somebody else feels the need or wish to deprive or disregard you. Unselfishness doesn't mean letting others walk all over you because they're in the mood to and it doesn't mean acting as if you don't count but everybody else does. If you don't take care of yourself and you go around believing that self-neglect means you're unselfish, your strategy is likely to bring bad consequences.

A person who lets himself be mistreated and says he doesn't mind always ends up feeling angry and resentful. He might for a long while say he doesn't care or say that it's okay if people treat him badly because he can take it. Or he might say the mistreatment is all right because his mother just can't help herself. He can even make himself feel *special* by congratulating himself for being so "unselfish" or tough. But I think this young person is heading for trouble if he does that. Inside, he's getting madder and madder about being treated badly and having no rights. Eventually, all that angry feeling is going to catch up with him. It may burst out in eruptions of rage; or he may get sick physically or get depressed or anxious. All these feelings and behaviors just mean he's sick of accepting mistreatment and he's trying to protest. He's trying to find a way to take care of himself again, to say his feelings matter—maybe not *more* than the next person's but just as much.

So if you're thinking you can get along pretty well just accepting mistreatment and saying it's okay, you don't mind because you're selfless and kind of special that way, you might want to rethink that strategy. It's not likely to work in the long run. It's the kind of strategy that's likely to leave you feeling lousy down the road and perhaps not understanding why you feel so bad. Unselfish people don't neglect themselves. They look after others' needs *in addition* to their own, not instead of their own. They don't say, "I don't matter." They say, "Other people matter, too." And they may say, "Everyone matters but sometimes I matter most *to me.*" That's only natural because everyone's "job one" is herself or himself.

Your right to look after yourself and to pay attention to your own needs is something that remains yours throughout your life. It is not a special right of childhood, or of adulthood. Your parents also have this right. They are entitled to do things for themselves. They needn't always put their children first. Good parents attend to their children's needs and try to satisfy them within reason, but they don't deprive themselves of all satisfactions in order to gratify their child's every wish. Take as an example a child who tells her mother, on the way home from school, that she wants to stop at a novelty store to buy some things for a party the next week. The mother says she doesn't want to stop at the store because she's had a long day at work and she still needs to prepare dinner for the family. The daughter asks whether her mother will take her to the store the next day. The mother considers the request but tells her daughter she'd planned to go to a once-yearly art show after work tomorrow; she'd been looking forward to the show for a long time. She offers to take her daughter shopping on Saturday. The daughter angrily complains that her mother is totally selfish.

If this mother always says "no" to her daughter's requests and puts her own plans first, the daughter might have a point. But perhaps that's not the case. Perhaps this is a case of a mother balancing her own wishes and needs with her daughter's. It's important for a parent to find that kind of balance. If she doesn't, she may end up resenting her daughter rather than loving and enjoying her. She'll also give her daughter the impression that adulthood is all work and no fun, which doesn't give her much to which she can look forward. And she will fail to teach her daughter that some amount of frustration is part of life.

Chapter 3

MISTREATMENT

Not all parents with problems mistreat their kids, but mistreatment is one of the things that can happen to kids when parents have problems. Mistreatment is anything a parent does that is seriously harmful to a child: to her body, or her mind, or her spirit, or her healthy development. Because they're not perfect, all parents occasionally mistreat their children. If you're lucky, you have a parent who notices when he's mistreating you and doesn't do the same thing again. He takes responsibility for his mistakes and learns from them. He's willing to apologize if he treats you badly. If you feel mistreated, you can talk to a good parent about it and your parent will listen and think about the sense in what you're saying.

Seriously troubled parents may mistreat their children and never take responsibility for their mistakes, no matter how much the child complains or explains her feelings. One of the harmful things about getting mistreated by parents who don't take responsibility is that young people can get confused about the kind of treatment to which they're entitled. They're not sure whether they're being mistreated or not. They *feel* mistreated but their parent says they're not.

The big, obvious forms of mistreatment, people sometimes call abuse. Examples are beating a child, or battering him with insulting comments, or making him do something that's clearly very bad for him (like trying a drug the parent is using or having sex when he's too young or the situation is inappropriate or he doesn't want to). Other forms of mistreatment or abuse are less obvious, but it's important for kids to recognize them, so I will discuss those as well. It's also important for kids to recognize when they're *not* being mistreated, because in the long run it's not helpful to claim you're abused when you're not

15

(we'll talk about that later, in Chapter Eight). Feeling abused *may* be a sign of actual abuse, but that's not always the case.

Let's talk more about what mistreatment and abuse are, both the obvious kinds and the more subtle kinds. Hurting another person's body or assaulting him with cruel words or depriving him of basic rights (like food and clothes and the right to move his body freely) is always abuse, even if the child has behaved badly. There is never "a good reason" for a parent to do any of these things to a child. Even if the child has been disrespectful or irresponsible or has mistreated the parent or someone else, that's no excuse for the parent to mistreat the child. Parents are adults who are supposed to model mature behavior, no matter how the child behaves; that's what parenting is about.

The more subtle or hidden kinds of mistreatment are harder to describe but important to understand. They usually have to do with mental or psychological pressure put on a child. For no good reason, the child is asked to give up opportunities to grow and develop in healthy ways. The child is made to feel that wanting those opportunities and trying for them is bad, selfish, or harmful to others. The child is asked to work against his own healthy growth. He is asked to act in ways that discourage growth and to give up activities that promote it, like when George's mother asks him to give up his excitement about going to camp. If she can't afford to send him to camp, therefore she tells him he won't be able to go, that's not mistreatment. But insisting he'll be miserable and lonely at camp, just like she was, is mistreatment. Another kind of mistreatment is when a child is made to feel bad for his legitimate feelings or sound ideas. Asking a child to work beyond his physical or mental capacity or in ways that may lead to physical harm or mental exhaustion is also mistreatment. An example would be requiring a child to move materials in and out of a hot fire or kiln when the child doesn't have the skills, strength or self-confidence and does not have proper safety gear. Asking a child to ride a horse she's not been adequately schooled to handle and does not want to ride would be another example.

How do you know when you're being mistreated? Not everything a parent asks of you that makes you angry or resentful is mistreatment. If your parent says you can't go out till you've cleaned your room, that's not abuse. You may not like it and you may not want to raise your own kids with that rule, but if it applies to all the cleaning-capable folks in the house (not the baby or the dog, that is) and if it's a rule you're told about in advance so you're not surprised by it just when you're all set to go out, then the rule's not a totally unreasonable one, is it?

One kind of abuse or mistreatment you can recognize is when you're asked to give up something that you enjoy even though you're not bringing harm to anyone. For example, you're asked to give up your interest in astronomy because your father thinks astronomy is "a stupid subject." Or to stop playing your accordion because your mother doesn't like the sound (even though you've offered to practice with your door closed, or when your mom is still at work). Or maybe you're asked to give up a fun and caring friend because your mother feels she was snubbed by your friend's mother. That's not fair. Your mother shouldn't take away your friendship to soothe her own hurt feelings.

A second kind of mistreatment is when a parent belittles a child and has no regard for the child's feelings. Say you're mad at your father for not giving you more spending money and you yell at him and say, "You're so stupid, I wish I had Jerry's father." Then your father shouts back, "You're such a damn idiot, I wish you weren't my son." If you complain about the mean comment your father's made, he says, "If you can dish it out, you'd better be able to take it, so stop your bellyaching." Sounds like a pretty messed-up interaction, doesn't it? You've said some rude and immature things to your father, but it's a parent's job to teach you; that is, to help you learn better ways of doing things, not to act as rudely and childishly as you have. A helpful parent might say to his rude child, "You can tell me what's bothering you without calling me names." Slinging mud back at you just shows you how *not* to be an adult, which isn't the kind of help kids need. A basically good parent who's often provoked by an angry and upset child may sometimes lose his temper and may occasionally say mean things back to the child, but the parent will strive not to retaliate when provoked and may apologize if he fails in that effort.

Let's go back to the clean-your-room-before-you-go-out rule to find another example of mistreatment. I've already said that a rule like that is not mistreatment. But what if your parents don't have a rule like that, and then suddenly when you're on your way out to a party they disapprove of, they invent a room-cleaning rule so that you're kept from your party. This behavior *is* mistreatment. Your parents are being dishonest and manipulative with you in order to get you to do what they want. If they have a good reason for not wanting you to go to the party (e.g., they think it's an unsafe situation), they should tell you that directly. New rules shouldn't be dreamed up to control your behavior.

When parents concoct meaningless rules just to control their children, rules lose their meaning. They're not there for the stated purpose, but for another, hidden purpose. The room-cleaning rule isn't really there because your parents believe your room should be neat; it's there so you won't go to the party. When your parent creates rules without thought, you lose faith in rules, and in your parents, and you feel helpless because you can't predict what the rules will be from one day to the next. You can't anticipate tomorrow's rules and prepare for them, for example, by cleaning your room in advance so you can go to your party.

Why do parents sometimes do things to kids or ask things of kids that are not good for them? There can be many reasons. Sometimes it's because the parent is immature and doesn't know how to communicate with a child who has a mind of his own. Or it may be that the parent doesn't care very much about the child's feelings and best interests but only cares about controlling the child's behavior.

Mistreatment sometimes occurs because the parent has a problem with his own feelings. Because of that problem, the child's behavior makes the parent uncomfortable, as if the child were rubbing a sore spot. The parent feels uncomfortable, perhaps without knowing why, and he wants to feel more comfortable. He senses he'll feel more comfortable if his child stops doing what he's doing, so he pressures the child to change. This may happen even when there's nothing wrong with what the child is doing. For example, maybe John is afraid of diving off a high dive and John's fear reminds his father of feeling like a coward or a sissy when the father was little. Instead of helping his child with his fear of diving, John's father insults the child. "You're such a crybaby," he taunts, "you must have got that from your mother." John's father is trying to manage his own shame by dumping it on his son.

As another example, suppose that June is a terrific gymnast. Her skills and medals remind her father about not having enough money for the gymnastics lessons he wanted when he was growing up. Instead of making peace with his own disappointment and enjoying June's success, June's father keeps forgetting to come home to give June a ride to gymnastics or he says he can't afford the lessons any more, even though he can.

June's father might realize that June's gymnastics interest is hitting a nerve for him, or he might not. He might just know he's irritable and he's forgetful about her lessons, but he doesn't know why. If he doesn't realize what's going on, but June does and she says, "Dad, it seems like my gymnastics is irritating some kind of sore spot with you," June's father might say, "Don't be ridiculous, that's the craziest thing I've ever heard. I just forgot once or twice, don't make a federal case out of it." That sort of response is hard on a child because she starts to question her own intuitions even when they're correct, as June's are. A healthy parent tries to realize if his child's behavior is making him uneasy for some reason of his own. He tries to work out or manage his own anxieties rather than blaming the child and asking the child to change when she's not doing anything wrong to begin with.

Let me bring in another idea: empathy. Empathy means being able to put yourself in another person's shoes so you can imagine what that person feels. For instance, a father notices that his son gets snappy and rude after a girl turns him down for a date; the father imagines the boy is feeling hurt and perhaps feeling lousy about himself and he's covering up those softer feelings with tough anger. Parents who don't have a lot of empathy for their kids are more likely to mistreat them, since they don't imagine how the mistreatment feels to the child.

Parents with problems are often short on empathy. Sometimes they have a capacity for empathy but, because of their problems, they just aren't using that empathy. It's like having hot water in the house but the tap is turned off. Other parents have never developed empathy; it's something that's simply in short supply in them. These people shouldn't have become parents in the first place, because it's impossible to be a good parent if you can't imagine your child's feelings. If you have a parent without empathy, you're likely to get a lot of mistreatment.

How is a child supposed to deal with mistreatment from a parent? If you can stop the mistreatment by talking to your parent, obviously that's the best thing. Or maybe you can get another adult to step in and talk to your parent for you. Parents who mistreat their kids only on occasion, perhaps when the parent is under stress, may respond positively when confronted about the mistreatment. Unfortunately, some parents don't respond well when their kids try to talk to them. They may try to listen but not really get the point, or they may get the point but they can't change their behavior, or they may get angry at the child for approaching them. Kids may find it especially difficult to get through to parents who inflict the subtler, more psychological kinds of mistreatment, the kinds that don't hurt your body but they hurt your spirit and self-esteem and they take away your respect for your parents. In these cases, the most important thing is something that sounds simple but often isn't. The most important thing is to know when you're being mistreated and to take a stand against it in your head, even if you can't stop it.

Often kids don't recognize mistreatment because it's scary and un-pleasant to think your parent is mistreating you. Sometimes it actually feels better to lie to yourself and say, "I deserved it." You may tell yourself you were rude or selfish or stupid or a smart aleck or too bossy or whatever. Since you love your parents (or at least want to love them) and hope they love you, it's hard to face bad things happening between them and you. But in the long run, it's healthier for you to recognize mistreatment than to blame it on yourself.

Another thing you can do if you're mistreated is to make up for your mother's or father's lack of empathy by giving yourself as much loving attention as you can. Try to be kind to yourself; try to treat yourself with respect and love. That doesn't mean spending all the money you can on expensive gifts for yourself. It means being understanding of your own feelings and difficulties, supportive of your own efforts, and pleased with your own accomplishments. It means treating yourself as you would treat a valued friend. It also means spending time with people other than your parents, who can give you encouragement and support.

As an example, think of Terry, whose father is always comparing him to his older brother, Donald. When Terry brings home his report card, his father scans the grades until he finds a subject in which Donald excelled. Then he'll say, "Donald always got A's in Science" (when Terry got a B). He doesn't say a word about Terry's A in English. If Terry says, "I got an A in English, Dad," his father just nods and doesn't even smile. If Terry comes home from a track meet with a ribbon for the 50-yard dash, his father says, "Donald won in the 50 *and* the 100." When his father makes these comments, Terry starts to get down on himself, to feel sad and irritable. But a strong, healthy part of Terry knows his father has a hang-up about Donald and knows that his father isn't giving him the recognition he deserves. So Terry congratulates himself for his successes and he makes a point of sharing his good news with two friends and a favorite schoolteacher, all of whom give him a deserved pat on the back.

Let's go back one more time to that question of what mistreatment is. Let's start again with the idea that all people have rights, kids included. They have the right to those things that are good for their own growth, development, and happiness, whenever those things don't cause harm to others. Does that mean you have a right to every dress, bike, or computer game that you want? No, it doesn't, not even if your parents can afford it. What it means is you have a right to have your own thoughts and feelings and to have them listened to and treated with respect. You have a right to have some control over your time too, so that it's not all spent doing what others would have you do, and some control over other things that belong to you, such as your space and possessions or money you've saved from working.

Ideas about possessions vary from culture to culture. In some cultures, people don't have private possessions, things they personally own. That's fine if you live in that type of culture or family. But if you live in a family in which certain things belong to certain people, then those rules should be respected. As an analogy, it's fine to play a basketball game with very few rules or a three page list of rules, but whatever rules are set should be honored by everyone playing the game. Otherwise players can't trust each other.

Here is an example of mistreatment that involves a parent not respecting a child's basic rights. Say you've made a friend at school. You like being with this friend because he's funny and smart and he listens to you and thinks you're good company. Spending time with this friend is good for you. It makes you happy and you learn things and you don't get into trouble when you're together. Say your father tells you to stop seeing this friend and you ask "why?" and your father says, "because I said so." When you say "give me a reason," your father says, "I said so, that's reason enough" or he says, "Because I work with his old man and I hate the guy's guts, that's why."

This story is an example of mistreatment that involves a parent not respecting a child's basic right to his own thoughts and feelings and his own life. You know that your friend is good for you, not bad for you. But your father isn't listening and isn't thinking about how giving up the friend will affect your life. Your father is thinking about himself and how he wants to punish the person he works with and dislikes. In this case, you may not be able to stop the mistreatment. You may not have a way to get your father to see your point. You may even have to give up your friendship, which would be sad. But whatever you do, it's important for you to know that your father ought not to have asked you to give up your friend.

Let's give a contrasting example. Say you have a new friend you enjoy and your mother says, "I don't want you visiting that child's house anymore because his older brothers both take drugs and I'm worried about you being exposed to that sort of thing. You might get pressured in ways you might not be ready to handle." In this case, you might not agree with your parent's views or feel happy about them, but your mother isn't mistreating you. She's thinking about your best interest, as she sees it, and taking your needs into consideration.

Neglect is another kind of mistreatment. It is another way of not respecting a child's feelings and thoughts, not by ridiculing them or opposing them, but by acting as if they don't exist or matter. If a parent doesn't attend to your need for clean clothes or healthy food or vaccinations, then he's acting as if these things that you need are not of importance, even though they are in fact very important in your life. You may think your parent has a "good reason" for not paying attention to your needs. Maybe he has a lot of worries of his own or he's depressed or very disorganized about getting things done, so you try to forgive him for neglecting your needs. But even if your parent really can't help himself, neglect is neglect and it's important to recognize it. It's important to know that your own needs aren't being met and that you have a right to have them met and to be angry and disappointed when they're not. If your parent isn't meeting your needs and can't be helped to do so, you may choose to turn to a friend's parent, a minister or a counselor for help. That's a smart thing to do.

Kids who get a lot of mistreatment from their parents sometimes feel selfish (remember *that* word) when they try to take the few good things their parents offer. That is, they try to take the good things and leave the bad ones. Even though that sounds like a very reasonable thing to do (which it is!), some kids feel, "If I'm mad at Dad and don't respect him and don't want to be like him, then I shouldn't take the food and clothes he buys me or learn what I can about baseball from him and show it off to my friends." Some kids get this feeling that they should take everything or nothing; they should accept their parents one hundred percent, or take nothing from them. They feel guilty and selfish if they take only what they want and reject the rest of what their parents want them to take. The situation is made even worse if your parent is the type who says, "You stay away if I've got nothing to offer you, but you sure come running home all sweet as pie the minute I've got something you can use."

As an example, imagine Taneesha whose mom often advises her not to worry about her friends' feelings. If Taneesha says, "Mary said I was stubborn," her mom says, "Don't worry about Mary. She doesn't know anything, she's a spoiled brat." But if Taneesha needs lunch money and her mother is short on cash, Mom will say, "Can't you get some off your friends?" If Taneesha says she's always borrowing from her friends and not paying back, which isn't right, her mother says, "They can afford it, you just get what you can from them." Taneesha rejects most of her mother's advice, since Taneesha believes in treating people fairly and not taking advantage of them. But when Taneesha needs help with her math, she feels guilty asking her mother even though her mother is a whiz with numbers. When Taneesha accepts her mother's math help, she feels bad about rejecting her mother's advice about friends. She feels even worse because her mother taunts her and says, "You sure get here fast and all nicey-nice when there's something I can do for you."

If you feel guilty taking only the good things from a difficult parent, your feelings are understandable, but let me suggest another way of thinking about the situation. Ask yourself *why* you are rejecting so many things that come from your parent. Are you rejecting good things or only those things that seem destructive and wrong-headed? If what you're rejecting is bad advice, confused ideas or hateful words, don't you think you *ought* to be rejecting those things, like Taneesha should? You're not doing it just for fun are you? In fact, I bet you'd rather your parent offered you good advice, clear ideas or kind words that you happily could accept. So don't fault yourself for throwing out the bad stuff and taking only the good stuff–that's the intelligent thing to do. Don't give yourself bad advice by saying, If you don't take the rotten stuff, then you shouldn't take anything at all. If we were talking about food, not parenting, that would be a good way to starve.

Chapter 4

WHEN A PARENT IS IN PAIN

Some kids have parents whose troubles are very painful; this chapter is especially for those kids. Parents in pain may cry a lot or seem fearful and restless. They may sleep too much or find it difficult to sleep at all. They may complain bitterly about things you don't understand and can't fix.

Some parents in pain confide in their kids telling them how sad or frightened they are, that they have no friends or talents, or even that they wish they were dead. Other suffering parents neglect their children or withdraw from them, or they become easily angered.

In writing this book I'm thinking mostly about the emotional problems and behavior problems parents can have, but many of the comments about parents in pain apply as well to parents with serious physical problems. Some physical problems lower a person's spirits, make him impatient and irritable, or reduce his physical abilities and strength. Like a parent in mental pain, he may be very focused on his suffering and unable to meet his child's needs. Other physical problems do not interfere with a parent's basic sense of well-being or with his parenting ability. Whether a parent can cope with physical problems without becoming a poor parent depends in part on the type of illness he has and in part on the type of person he is. One parent with a severe disability or difference, for example, a spinal cord injury, might make an excellent parent, while another parent with a minor disability, for example, a missing finger, might be preoccupied with the difference so that it interferes greatly with parenting.

One thing that's hard about having a parent in pain is that you may feel very sorry for your parent, as sorry as you might feel for a suffering baby or a helpless, sick animal. If you've been close to your parent, it can feel unbearable to see him suffer and not know how to help. You feel small and powerless. You may struggle inside trying to figure out whether there's something you can do to take away your parent's pain.

For example, Sheila's mother has been deeply depressed for months. She doesn't go out of the house. Often, she lies in her bed in the dark, even in the middle of the day, or she sits rocking in a chair, wrapped up in a shawl like an old woman. She barely eats or talks. Sometimes, she sobs for a while or suddenly snaps at Sheila about making noise. Sheila feels frightened and distressed by her mother's suffering. Over and over, she asks her mother to eat and tries to get her to dress and go out for a walk. She tries talking to her about things that used to interest her, to see if she'll come to life. But nothing works, so Sheila feels more and more hopeless.

Some parents in pain give kids the message, "This is my problem— there's no way for you to help." That message may not leave you feeling good because it shuts you out and it says you're powerless; but the positive thing about that message is at least it doesn't encourage false ideas about what you can do to relieve a parent's pain.

Other parents do not communicate to their kids much at all. A former soldier with post-traumatic stress disorder might be caught up in his or her suffering and leave the child's care to the other parent or leave the child to care for herself. The child may feel as if she's ceased to exist for her parent, as if she's been forgotten and barely matters. She's also left to figure out on her own what might be going on with her suffering parent, because no one is talking to her about what's wrong. She may feel shut out and feel that her parent doesn't trust her with whatever is so troubling. An air of secrecy may fill the home and lead a child to disturbing fantasies about the parent. For example, the child of an ex-soldier with PTSD might worry about what the parent did during the war, or what happened to him or her. Knowing the truth about the parent's experiences often would be less difficult than being left to fantasy, because the truth can be discussed and a well-functioning parent can help a child digest even painful truths.

Some parents encourage their kids to feel overly responsible to relieve the parent's unhappiness. One type of parent guilt-trips the child, saying, "If only you didn't spend so much time off with your friends, I wouldn't feel so depressed." That parent encourages the child to make false connections between the parent's suffering and the child's activities. It's not true that the parent's depression comes from the child's social activity, but the parent uses that false connection to push the child to feel guilty. Another parent may plead with a child, begging him to "help me, please help me," as if the child were a very powerful person (more powerful than all the adults around). However, the child is not powerful and cannot help.

Another message a child may get is that he is so special to the parent that he alone can help. This child is saddled with an uncomfortable, unrealistic sense of power and importance. But it is a confusing sense of power because nothing he actually does to try to help his parent does much good. Maybe Dad puts on some clothes and goes to work for a day or two, but then he goes back to moping around the house. Maybe Mom says, "Thank you, Dear, I always feel better when I talk with you," but then she's up pacing all night, anxious and restless as always. So the child ends up feeling powerless, even though the parent acted as if that child could do so much for him or her.

If your parent acts as if only you can understand him and help him, he's telling you that you're special—not in the everyday, real ways that you actually are special, but in some magic way that's hard to define. You may be tempted to accept this idea of being the only one who can understand and help, because it does make you feel special, which may feel good. But in the end, accepting that idea gets you in trouble, first because it's not realistic and, second, because lots of responsibilities inappropriate to a child or teen go with it.

Kids with parents in pain can have a hard time leading their own everyday lives and doing the things that are appropriate for kids their age. Even if your parent hasn't told you that you need to stay home and help him, it can be hard to go off to camp or the beach or even to school or a job when you're worried about how your parent is doing at home. You may feel guilty if you're having fun or if you're learning things and accomplishing things that can make you a happy, successful person. You may think, "How can I let myself be happy when my mom's at home talking crazy talk to the wall, or my dad's out drinking away his problems?"

Sometimes kids with very troubled, suffering parents feel they are different from other kids. They feel set apart from others because there's something awful going on in their lives. They may try to pretend they like being special by taking great pride in being "deep" or "sensitive." Having a suffering parent can make you deep and sensitive in some ways and it's okay to take a bit of pride in that, but it's best not to use that pride to hide from the sadder, more worried feelings about having an experience that's different from most of your peers' experiences. It's better to pay attention to those feelings so you can go about the business of realizing that having a troubled parent doesn't mean you're a Martian who's not a member of the human race; it just means you've got some tough things to deal with.

Even though you may be having some unusual experiences, you're not basically different from others. It will be good for you to spend time away from home and to get to know other kids' parents. In the long run, getting too well adapted to living with a suffering person won't help you. It will make it hard for you to move into other, more normal situations, where people aren't suffering all the time. Kids who get too isolated in a home where there's constant suffering can feel out-of-place in ordinary settings. They're like combat soldiers who have trouble adapting when the war is over and it's time to return to ordinary life. Combat survivors and survivors of disturbed families all may feel they can't identify with people who haven't had the experiences they have, and they may feel that no outsider can relate to the world they've known so well.

The best way to avoid these problems is to broaden your world while you're still at home dealing with your troubled parent. Don't hole up in your unhappy home until it's time to leave to go away to college, the army or a job. Try not to feel disloyal to your parent if you seek out and enjoy other adults' company; keep in mind that you have room in your heart for many relationships. Adding new ones is a healthy part of growing up and needn't mean giving up your old ties. You can keep old ties or give them up depending on whether they're worth preserving. If you do lessen or give up your tie to your father, it's not because you made friends with Morris's father; it's because of problems between you and your dad.

Another concern for some kids of suffering parents is a feeling they get that the more successful they are, the bigger the gap between them and their unhealthy parent. The only thing Sara's mother likes to talk to Sara about is misery and failure. But Sara is a high-spirited young woman who has lots of successes and happy, exciting moments in her life. When she tries to tell her mother what a great time she had galloping on a horse or how awesome she felt winning her chess competition, her mother seems bored or irritable and she quickly changes the subject to talk about her own ill-health or to tell Sara that horseback riding may aggravate her old knee injury. It's sad but true that, for some kids, having happy or excited feelings, or doing well in life, can leave them feeling like a stranger to their own parent. That kind of alienation is an uncomfortable, even scary experience. You want your parents to feel glad you're doing well and to join in your pleasure and competence, but they don't.

Becoming sad and miserable like your parent, or crazy or anxious like her, may at times feel like some sort of solution to your problem. If you are sad like your mom or overly focused on illness like she is, you won't have to feel guilty for enjoying yourself while she's miserable. And you may feel close to her again since you share some of her feelings. She may even show more interest in you if you're like her, since misery loves company. She may think you're special because you're so sensitive to her suffering and you suffer yourself. However, choosing that route means giving up your own growth and development and your pleasure in life, and that's a huge price to pay.

Unfortunately, some religions idealize suffering. These religions can add to guilt over preferring joy and lightness of spirit to sadness and worry. Religions may also teach that suffering individuals are superior and deserve special admiration. People come to believe that unless they suffer a great deal, they are plain and ordinary, perhaps of lesser value. I don't agree with these ideas. Some suffering is inevitable in life and will come to everyone because everyone deals with illness, loss, and distress. But to seek suffering and devalue joy does not to me seem like a good use of one's time on earth.

Kids with a suffering parent can feel very afraid of what will happen to that parent: Maybe your father will commit suicide or end up in a mental hospital or he will die and leave you fatherless. In some cases, it's realistic to feel a parent may end up dead or hurt. If your parent is terribly depressed or keeps driving while drunk, it's realistic to worry he'll be killed in an accident. But your worrying won't keep bad things from happening, so give yourself a break from it whenever you can. If your mother takes an overdose while you're at school, you're no more responsible if you were having fun at school than if you were sitting at school worried sick about Mom. Worrying has no power to keep bad things from happening. It won't keep your airplane from crashing or your mother from taking pills. And worrying a lot doesn't make you a better person. Worrying so much that you stay home from school is no solution either. Going to school is your job. It's your responsibility and you shouldn't give it up to look after someone else's jobs and responsibilities.

If you have a suffering parent, you may feel concerned that your parent's sadness or sickness will suck you in, so you will end up feeling awful or getting sick too, and you and your parent will both be in a big pit you'll never get out of. The worry about getting sucked in by your parent's pain or her unreasonable fears is one you can help yourself with by thinking about the worry and trying to understand it. Another person's depression or anxiety isn't really a big vacuum cleaner that can suck you in, so what is it you're really scared about?

Maybe you're worried you inherited something bad from a parent (we'll talk about that later). Or maybe you feel your parent's suffering is leading you to tough questions about God or the value of life and those questions feel overwhelming (which means you could benefit from some help with them from a wise adult). Or maybe you're finding it hard to live in "two worlds"–the world of your parent's suffering and the playfulness of your school buddies, for example–so it seems like it would be easier just to join your parent in his world and not feel so painfully separated from him. That last idea is not about being *sucked in;* it's about making a choice that might seem like a good solution at the moment but probably won't in the future. Try to remember that no matter how bad you may feel at times, life is long and gives almost endless opportunities for getting better and feeling better. Remember as well that help is available when it's needed.

What can a kid do if he has a suffering parent? You can try to be helpful and considerate to a parent in pain but also try to be realistic about what you can and can't do to help. You're not an adult and you're not a psychiatrist or a physician. You can't make your mother better. She has to do that herself, with the help of other adults. So try not to get down on yourself for only helping a little and try not to get down on yourself for having your own needs and wishes, which may be very different from your parent's. Try to stick with your own responsibilities to do what you need to in order to grow up healthy.

Allow yourself plenty of time away from your sick parent. Don't give up on your education or your friendships or on taking care of your own health and safety. The healthy part of your parent will want to see you grow up to be strong and happy.

Sometimes kids whose parents are sad and weak for a long time will get very tough with their parents. They'll feel disgusted with them and become unsympathetic and angry. Partly, the kids are acting that way because their parent's sadness or worries frighten them. It's more comfortable to think that the parent is a bad, rotten person than to think the parent has a grief or mental disorder that won't go away. It's also exhausting and depressing to live with someone who is suffering or out of control and is seldom fun.

Sometimes kids get tough and provocative with sad or sick parents because they hope their parents will buck up and defend themselves if they're under attack. Kids may do this kind of attacking without knowing why they're doing it. They do it because their instinct tells them one way to get someone out of the doldrums is to give them something real to worry about. If you kick a dog that's stuck in the brambles, the kick may be more painful than the brambles and will get him moving. Or so the reasoning goes. Occasionally, this type of strategy works for a little while, but usually it just makes for arguments between kids and parents and not for lasting solutions to a parent's problems. Hard as it is, kids have to try to accept that they can't provide those lasting solutions.

Having a constantly sad or anxious parent is very threatening to a child. There's no way around that. Kids want to feel that when they have problems of their own, their parents can help them find solutions. It's very hard on a young person when a parent can't solve his own problems and when he suffers a lot. Unhappy parents make kids worry about growing up. Kids worry they'll be sad or sick when they grow up (which need not be the case). They also may feel bad about wanting to grow up and leave home, because they're afraid their parent won't be all right when the young person is gone. The truth is, if your parent is sad, anxious or psychotic, he's not likely to be any worse off when you grow up than he is now. His pain doesn't have to do with you being little or big, home or away. It has to do with something inside your parent that your parent has to work out.

 **Chapter 5**

WHEN A PARENT CAUSES PAIN

Sara's mother sings Gospel songs with Sara's sisters while they gather around the piano. If Sara tries to join in on a song, her mother tells her, "Hush, you can't carry a tune like us so keep your mouth shut."

Once or twice a month, Tim's father comes home drunk and tells his gay son how repulsive he is. Sometimes, he smacks his son and tells him he needs someone to beat some manliness into him.

Kim's mother locks her in the closet in the dark if she's done something her mother disapproves of, like using a swear word or wearing a sweater her mother says is too tight.

Carmen's father slips into the bathroom when she's showering so he can see her without clothes. Sometimes he touches her sexually and comments on her body.

Whenever she's having a bad day, Charles' mother tells him he'll never amount to anything. He's the spitting image of his father, that worthless sonofabitch who abandoned her years ago.

In this chapter, I want to talk about kids whose parents do things that are obviously hurtful, kids whose parents set out to hurt them, physically or emotionally. All kids whose parents deliberately hurt them have certain things in common. One thing they have in common is lots of anger. Anger can take many forms and we'll look more closely at those in the next chapter. Here I'll simply say that all kids who are hurt feel deeply angry. In fact, a stronger word like fury or hate might be a better choice, because deliberate abuse by a parent makes for powerful, even overwhelming, anger.

It's not pleasant to feel fury or hatred toward a parent. Affection and respect feel better than anger and hate. Unfortunately, you don't have the option to feel affection and respect for someone who is hurting you. You may pretend to have those feelings. You may even fool yourself into thinking you do. But you can't really enjoy or appreciate what hurts you. It's human nature to feel anger at what hurts us. It's also human nature to want to hurt others when we've been hurt. You may not act on those wishes, but you'll feel them. Forget all the pretty ideas about ties of blood. Love comes from loving interactions, not from ties of blood. Abuse brings hate and anger.

Kids with lots of hate for abusive parents may fight the hate that's inside them. Hatred is tough to bear. It tires you out and makes you wonder about yourself. Some kids with lots of hate feel as if they're bad people, even monsters. They wonder if they're capable of loving feelings or only of angry, destructive feelings. They may go to church or synagogue or to a mosque and hear about love, compassion, and forgiveness. Then they look inside and see hate and anger and they wonder if Jesus or the imam or their friends could possibly love and respect them when they've got so much anger inside.

If you are a kid like that, it's important to remember that it's right and natural to hate what hurts you. You're not feeling hate because of being a bad or basically hateful person. If one of your friends moved into your house and was abused, she would feel the hate and anger you feel. You can try and understand what's wrong with your abusive parent and why he's so disturbed and destructive. That understanding may soften your anger a little, but don't ask yourself to accept the abuse itself and try hard not to condemn your reasonable anger about being mistreated. Your anger doesn't mean you're bad or incapable of love. It means you're reacting the way nature intended you to react to being hurt. For the time being, you're stuck being angry because you're stuck with mistreatment. The anger isn't due to your nature—it's due to your situation.

A young person may try to get away from his anger by saying to himself, "The abuse is my fault, not my parent's." You tell yourself that if you weren't so opinionated or messy or sexually developed or such a slow reader (or such a fast reader), then your parent wouldn't mistreat you. Or maybe you are gay or fat or have a crooked leg or you have unusual interests, so you tell yourself the mistreatment is your fault because you're different from other kids and your parent has reason to be upset. This kind of thinking helps you escape your anger. It also helps you escape the pain of accepting that your parent is a poor parent who has big limitations around loving and around behaving in mature ways. It's tough to accept a parent's limitations, especially if they are very large, which is always the case with abusive parents. Sometimes it feels better to say, "It's my fault, not Dad's." That way you protect your positive image of Dad. You may also feel less helpless about the abuse because you tell yourself all you have to do is shape up and the mistreatment will stop. That's not true but it may help you feel better.

You may be asking, if there are so many advantages to believing the abuse is your fault, not Dad's or Mom's, why *not* believe it? The big reason not to believe it is because it's not true and believing things that aren't true often has major negatives that accompany it sooner or later. The biggest negative about believing this untruth is that you are left feeling you are a bad person who deserves abuse. If you carry that belief into adulthood, you may seek out relationships with people who will hurt you just like your parent hurt you, and you may run away from people who want to treat you well, which is what happens with the young man in this example:

For years, Julian's father told him what a clumsy, brainless ox he was. Julian's father said he must have had the worst luck on earth to get a kid like his. Julian fled from the anger this mistreatment bred. He accepted his father's negative messages and made them part of his self-image. As a young adult, he walked around with slumped posture and a mumbling voice and he always thought of himself as stupid, even though he in fact was bright and creative. A young woman, Doris, took a liking to him when she saw his work in their painting class and heard his thoughtful comments about art. But Julian shied away from Doris. Her admiration for him made him uncomfortable. He didn't know how to respond to it. Some months later, Julian was walking down the street and he tripped over a raised square of sidewalk and fell. A young woman walking alongside him approached him and said, "Not too coordinated, eh?" Julian instantly felt at home with this woman, JoAnn, who was quick to find fault with him and never noticed his unusual creativity or intelligence. He started asking her out on dates.

There's a second problem with accepting the idea that you've deserved or caused the abuse you receive: you may end up feeling like you have some kind of big, monster power to provoke people to violence or to soothe them, so you walk around worrying about how you're using all that power. That power (which you don't really have—it's a fantasy) will be a burden to you. You'll feel like you would if you always had a loaded gun in your pocket. You'll feel that you have to be awfully careful around people or your monster power will be set off and hurt someone. You'll likely be afraid to be assertive and to stand up for yourself, because you'll confuse assertiveness with dangerous aggression.

Often kids who have been sexually abused believe they have some type of extraordinary sexual power that makes adults lose control of their sexual wishes. The kids feel they have to hide their bodies or their faces so that their sexuality won't overpower the people around them. This idea is incorrect. Adults who sexually abuse children or teens are not overpowered by any special sexiness of the child. These adults have something wrong with them. They are lacking in normal self-control and lacking in other ways as well. A great many children are lovely and attractive. No matter how attractive a child is, that attractiveness is never the reason an adult abuses the child. If a child wrongly takes responsibility for the sexual abuse she (or he) suffers, the child will feel she shouldn't ever show off or enjoy her body. That's a shame, since the child is entitled to enjoy her (or his) attractiveness, which is not the cause for the abuse. Often a child who has been sexually abused will gain or lose weight in order to hide her body's natural shape and to look unattractive, or she will dress badly or mistreat her body by injuring or scarring it. These things hold true both for boys and for girls who are victims of sexual abuse.

Sexual abuse often brings extraordinarily distressing feelings. These feelings can include powerful urges to hurt others, to hurt oneself or to commit suicide. The violation of trust associated with sexual abuse is massive, as is the sense of being soiled, humiliated, helpless, and forever changed. These feelings can be so disturbing that a child trying to cope with them alone is in real danger of self-harm, both physical and psychological. Kids who have experienced sexual abuse need a great deal of emotional support. If you have experienced sexual abuse, you should try to overcome the shame and fear you may feel and ask a trusted adult for help.

Let's look at a couple examples of a parent who deliberately causes emotional pain. Cecilia's mother always told Cecilia, "You're driving me crazy." She also liked to say, "You'll be the death of me" and to ask, "What have I done to deserve this aggravation?" She said these things from the time Cecilia was a baby and said them over the smallest things, like when the child talked loudly or got her shoes dirty. Anyone watching and listening to Cecilia's mother would see that she was striving to create pain in her child. Deliberately inflicting pain on another and enjoying that experience is called *sadism*. A parent who regularly shows sadism to a child is an enemy to that child. A child whose parent is her enemy is a child in danger. A second example of sadism is the woman who walks in on her adolescent son when he's undressed and stares at him, noting with enjoyment the extreme discomfort she is causing.

Instead of recognizing her mother's sadism and rejecting her mother's extreme reactions, Cecilia accepted the idea that she was the cause of her mother's unhappiness and tantrums. She grew up feeling she was a bad person who had to be careful about every breath she took, lest she upset someone. She denied that her mother actually took pleasure in having tantrums and saw her mother as a victim of difficult and ungrateful children.

It's a tall order for a young child to reject the distorted ideas a parent pushes on him. It's not easy for an older child either, but when you're older you have a better chance of knowing what's reasonable and what's not since you've had more experience out in the world than a small child has. In the long run, it's always healthier to stay with the truth about your parent, even when the truth is awful. If your parent deliberately does things to hurt you, the truth is that you have a very troubled parent who is treating you badly. Your parent is not trustworthy and is not a mature adult. Even if your own behavior at times is provocative, childish or mean, your behavior is not the cause of your parent's abusiveness. The cause is within your parent. Though it's always a good idea to work on whatever shortcomings you have as a person, try to understand that your limitations are not the reason you are being abused.

Another reason it's tough to accept that your parent is deliberately hurting you is that accepting that fact can lead you to some serious questions about life. You may wonder why God lets you suffer mistreatment or you may wonder if all people deep down are bad or whether it's worthwhile getting attached to people. I said earlier that one thing abused kids have in common is anger. Another is mistrust. The mistrust is there for good reason because kids are born to put a great deal of trust in adults and when that trust is broken, deep doubt naturally develops.

Suzi grew up with two parents who regularly belittled her and occasionally hit her or deprived her of food and other necessities, such as bus money for getting to school or toiletries she needed in order to be clean and well groomed. Suzi also suffered sexual abuse by an uncle. As she went through her teen years, Suzi started to act tough and to seem indifferent to others' feelings. Occasionally, she was aggressive and threatening to her peers. When people offered her kindness, Suzi's attitude was, "Forget it, man, whatever you're selling, I'm not buying." She told herself everyone was a con. No one really cares about anyone. She could do just fine on her own, relying on her street smarts. She didn't need friends. She certainly didn't need family. Although Suzi told herself she wasn't interested in other people and didn't care to depend on them, she actually was terrified to trust people because she had been so badly let down by the people who should have been her biggest supporters.

No easy answers exist to the big questions about God and life that can come from abuse by a parent, but one thing that may help is to look around and notice people other than the ones who are hurting you. Try not to give up on *all* people. Instead, let yourself see that many people treat each other with consideration and respect. Opening your eyes to that broader reality may hurt at first: If your father treats you like garbage, you may feel even sadder and more angry about that if you see that your friend Harry's father treats him with kindness. But it's tremendously important to know that people can connect in positive ways. Even though you may never have that kind of connection with your abusive parent, you can have it with your friends or teachers, and some day with your own partner, children and coworkers. That's why it's best not to pretend that the whole world is just like your abusive father, mother, or stepfather. That kind of pretending protects you a bit from the pain of feeling deprived, but it keeps you from turning to others for better relationships. If you believe everyone in the world is dangerous and cruel, you will be left taking the attitude, "I don't need anyone but myself; I don't care about anyone but myself." That kind of attitude makes for a lonely life and a deep-down feeling of fear and insecurity.

Another way people sometimes cope with abuse is to "get into it," by which I mean they accept and even play up the role of the abused or deprived person. They think of being abused as a special status and they try to squeeze some advantage from it, for example, by acting as if the world "owes them," so they're entitled to anything they can get by any means. Mary has this kind of attitude. She likes to shoplift and she tells herself she's entitled to take what she can get because she didn't get from her mother what her friends got from theirs.

Mary's attitude isn't hard to understand, but it's not good for her in the long run to take the attitude of being "owed." She stops playing by the rules of society, which means she may end up in trouble with the law. She's a poor friend and coworker because she's always thinking about what she can get, not what she can contribute. And stealing things from stores doesn't really relieve the pain of not getting love from her mother. Feeling special because of being abused doesn't do a lot for her self-esteem in the long run, either. She feels she can't compete with others as an equal. She can only compete if she adopts the special status of victim.

Another abused child, Antonio, manages by getting overly fond of the idea of being a martyr, that is, someone chosen, like Jesus, to bear heavy burdens. He tells himself he's special because he's suffered so much pain. When Antonio grows up and leaves his abusive family, he may keep finding ways to expose himself to more abuse. His self-esteem has become dependent on being a martyr, so if he's not suffering, he feels like a nobody. In order to become healthy and happy, he will need to discover that he can be a regular person, not a martyr, and still be admired and loved, by others and by himself.

Some parents behave pretty decently much of the time, but every once in a while they become abusive, perhaps through sudden or severe ridicule. Having an intermittently abusive parent can be very confusing. It's easier to know what to feel toward a constantly abusive person. It's easier to know it makes sense to hate them or want them out of your life. But if your parent is generally okay (maybe at times he's even generous and fun), but every once in a while he does something seriously hurtful, then you may try especially hard to deny your anger and protect the good parts of the relationship.

The truth is that even if abuse only occurs from time to time, it will bring angry and distressed feelings. If it occurs every once in a while over a long period of time, so that you always know it's going to happen again sooner or later, it will affect your entire relationship, even when things are peaceful. Your trust in your parent is damaged and won't restore itself just because your mother hasn't hurt you in a while. It's like living beside a volcano that erupts every two or three years. You want to keep your distance. You don't trust that mountain. You know it's only a matter of time before it blows again. Trust is restored only when a parent really changes, which means she realizes her behavior is wrong, she takes steps to become a person who no longer abuses others, even when stressed, and she apologizes to those she's harmed and tries to help them recover.

Chapter 6

PARENTS IN POVERTY

Poverty can be absolute or relative. Absolute poverty means that the person would be considered impoverished in any culture. Lack of adequate food, clean water, basic medical care, shelter and clothing define poverty around the world. Relative poverty means that a person has much less than the people in the surrounding community, but may have his basic needs met. Absolute poverty is always a problem for kids because it leads to physical suffering, possible growth and development problems, even death. Relative poverty may or may not be a big problem for a child. In this chapter, we'll look at what can make it a problem.

Many situations can lead to one or the other kind of poverty in a family. Poverty is most often linked to lack of paid employment. When a parent loses a job and cannot find another, when a parent's health deteriorates so he cannot work, when a parent has no childcare and thus cannot work, when the entire community is poor and jobs are scarce, when a parent is unwilling to work for one reason or another . . . all these circumstances may lead to poverty. Some families are fortunate because they have money set aside from earlier employment, or from inheritance, so they can get through periods of unemployment without becoming poor. Other families feel the impact of poverty quickly when a parent or parents have no employment or have a low paying job.

The effects of poverty on children are many. Absolute poverty brings severe hardship due to effects such as hunger, thirst, illness, lack of protection from harsh weather, and lack of a home and access to a school. Both absolute poverty and relative poverty bring complicated emotions for kids. Children in poverty understandably feel let down by their parents. Children look to parents to provide well for them and when parents do not do so, kids are disappointed. Often they feel angry with the parent. The anger may be more intense if the child feels that a parent could do more to make money for the family than he or she is doing. But even if the child knows the parent has a real disability or has looked hard for a job but cannot find one, it still is natural to feel some anger toward a parent who does not provide for one's needs. A child might think, "You shouldn't have had kids if you couldn't provide for us."

A child's anger may depend in part on how the other families in the community are faring. This is true especially for older children and teens who are quite aware of how their friends and schoolmates live. A child in a poor family within a poor community may resent her parents less than a child in a poor family within a wealthy community. The second child may not understand why her parents can't make money when it seems like everyone else's parents can. She may feel that her parents aren't trying as hard as they might, or that something is wrong with her parents. She may feel ashamed of her parents and that shame may pile on top of shame over having fewer nice clothes than schoolmates, or a basement apartment instead of a big house with a lawn. She may have to make excuses when invited places that cost money or require transportation or if a gift is expected and her family can't manage to purchase it. All of these circumstances are particularly hard on teenagers, because most teenagers are already working hard to feel secure among peers.

Some kids will be fortunate enough to find friends who don't judge them based on their possessions or their parents' wealth, but not all kids will have that good fortune. So poorer kids may also suffer from discrimination by their peers, especially if poverty is not common in their community.

Poverty can also bring great insecurity. A child worries about getting enough to eat or about ending up in a shelter or in foster care. Or he worries about not having money for the bus fare to get home from school or for the school field trip. A teacher may ask kids to bring in a few dollars for a field trip without knowing that one child in the class immediately feels stressed about whether he will have the money. A poor child knows that the TV service or even the electricity or phone may be cut off if his parents don't get a bill paid on time.

Most kids in poverty will complain to their parents about what they feel they are lacking. Some impoverished parents do an excellent job of explaining their circumstances and reassuring their kids, as much as the reality will allow. For example, a child might complain that all her friends have iPhones and she doesn't. Her dad might tell her that he understands that teenagers often like to have the things they see their friends owning or wearing, but he cannot afford an iPhone since he has been out of work for many months, so she will have to do without it. He may remind her that having fancy possessions is not the most important thing in life and that any friend who would think less of her for not having an iPhone isn't that good a friend. If he has more money in the future, he might consider getting her an iPhone, but not necessarily. There may be more important things for the family to purchase or to save for.

Kids in poverty who see others around them with more wealth, possessions, and security may feel a great deal of envy. Envy is a natural response to the situation, but it's not a good feeling to get stuck on for too long. Envy is painful, so feeling it is not fun. Envy involves hateful feelings toward those who have more than you. Again, it's natural, but not pleasant and it doesn't get you anywhere. Envy is also passive. It means sitting back feeling resentment. Instead of getting stuck in envy, you'd likely feel better focusing on what you can do to improve your situation now or in the future. Then you won't feel so helpless or hopeless.

An example of a teen overcoming envy is Anna, whose family seldom has an extra dime and sometimes has to do without quality food, phone service, and holiday gifts for a period of time. For much of the school year, when Anna had to say 'no' to friends wanting to go to the movies (because she had no money), she felt angry and envious. Later in the year, she started thinking ahead to the next summer, when she would be sixteen and could look for a summer job that would give her spending money. That idea pleased her and relieved her envy and frustration.

Kids in poverty need to know that their future, as adults, need not be limited by poverty. A child can do things to increase his chances of having an adult life in which his needs will be met. The most important thing he can do is to concentrate on school and plan to graduate high school, then go on to college or a trade school. Even kids whose families cannot help them with higher education can get that education. Scholarships, loans, and work-study programs are available to help kids in tight financial circumstances. Kids whose parents are poor might also want to get to know financially successful adults in order to pick up ideas from those adults about how to prepare for a more financially secure future. School is extremely important. A positive attitude toward work as a way to make money and also to get satisfaction is also very important.

One note of caution for kids in poverty. It's hard not to see money as the most important thing in the world when you don't have enough of it. But happiness really does not depend on wealth. It is important to have enough money to meet basic needs, but tons of extra money won't add tons of happiness to your life. So don't lose sight of the other things that bring happiness: friends, family, work, hobbies, nature, and so forth. And don't let the desire for money lead you down a bad path, for example, the path of selling drugs. That choice might bring fast money but it very likely will bring big new problems into your life.

Chapter 7

PARENTS WITH DIFFICULT PERSONALITIES

When Parents Hurt Through Helping (the Overprotective Parent)

I've talked primarily about abuse and neglect, but parents who over-protect can also create real challenges for their kids. I'm thinking about parents who see danger around every corner, who are quick to expect that a person's efforts will bring bad outcomes. An outsider looking at an overprotective parent may see the parent as unusually concerned, involved, and loving, but the child of an overprotective parent may have difficulty. He may feel smothered by his parent, who is always hovering and keeping an eye on everything he does. He may also feel that his parent takes the joy out of life by constantly predicting trouble and failure.

Louise, thirteen, wants to go on a two-day class trip that involves a night of camping out. She asks her mom and her mom's face immediately registers a worried and disapproving expression very familiar to Louise. Without asking the particulars of the plan or how Louise feels about it, her mom starts to detail all the things that could go wrong on the trip. She worries about the weather forecast, about the chaperones, about boys and girls camping out near to each other, about mosquitoes, and about campsite vandalism. On and on goes the list of potential problems. She says nothing at all about the fun Louise could have. When Louise tries to redirect her by mentioning how much she likes s'mores and campfires, Mom says, "S'mores taste good but they're so sticky, and sometimes the smoke around a campfire can be awful. Your hair smells of it for a week."

Louise may have many challenges in dealing with her mom's attitude. She may feel her own spirits fall as she absorbs her mom's negativity. She may start to lose her enthusiasm for the camp-out and wonder why she thought it would be fun. Her mood begins to mirror her mom's. Life seems less hopeful and exciting. She now feels frightened of the trip and feels out of sync with her friends who are excited about the adventures they'll have camping out. Louise thinks of opting to stay home, but now feels ashamed over her fearfulness and worried about how she's going to make it in life if she can't try new things. Suddenly, she feels she has no good options and she becomes anxious and has trouble sleeping. She goes to her mother to complain about her sleeplessness and her mother offers her sleeping medicine.

Another child might respond more rebelliously than Louise to an overprotective parent. Juan's dad always worries about his son getting hurt. He doesn't want Juan involved in any sports that bring even the slightest chance of injury. He gives Juan an early curfew and keeps a close eye on him. Juan reacts by arguing with his dad and telling him he's an old man and a worrywart. He says he's going to do what he wants, no matter what his dad says. His dad's worry and his warnings increase.

Though Juan insists that he will defy his dad and do what he wants, underneath his bravado he is increasingly worried. His father's warnings are undermining his confidence. If his dad doesn't think he can play sports safely, maybe he can't. And since his dad is against his participating in sports, his dad won't be there to support him if he does have trouble or gets hurt. He'll be on his own. He won't even want to tell his dad what he's doing.

Juan's story makes it clear that an exceptionally worried and overprotective parent can leave a child feeling insecure and also alone with his endeavors. Juan would have felt better and had more success had his dad given a balanced view of sports, showed confidence in his son, and promised to be there to enjoy his efforts and to help him over any obstacles.

A child or teen with an overprotective parent likely will feel angry at the parent and also guilty and insecure. The depressing weight of the parent's worry produces anger, as does the experience of having to fight through the parent's objections every time the child wants to do something new or different. The worried parent never opens the door for the child and invites him out into the world. He closes the door and warns of dangers on the other side. The child must fight his way out on his own—or stay inside.

Guilt over anger or rebelliousness may trouble a child because his parent's destructive behavior is dressed as concern. That concern is emotionally confusing too, because the child likely feels impeded, not loved, yet the parent insists he is acting out of concern. Insecurity comes from absorbing some of the parent's worry and negativity and from feeling alone and unsupported when out in the world. The child often experiences his parent as someone who stays home and worries and does not accompany the child as he ventures out. That accompaniment is very important to a child's sense of comfort in the broader world. With a parent at his side, a child can feel happy and safe in the world outside the home. But if the parent stays home, portrays the outside world as dangerous, and requires the child either to stay home or to go out alone, then the challenges of the outside world seem great.

Complicated emotions may lurk behind a parent's worry and protectiveness. An overprotective parent may have fears of her own anger at her child and she may unconsciously believe that her anger will harm that child. The real danger she fears is the danger she herself poses to the child, but she does not understand herself well enough to know this. She projects her own dangerousness onto the big bad world beyond the home and works overtime to protect her child from it. This mother needs help understanding that all parents feel angry at times with their children. The anger is okay and can be managed in ways that won't hurt a child. It doesn't have to be denied and hidden behind concern and worry.

Another possibility with a worried, overprotective parent is that she can't stand the idea of her child growing up. For her, to grow up and become independent means to grow apart emotionally and lose all the closeness of the early mother-child relationship. She can't imagine being close to her child in new ways as that child becomes more mature and capable. And she can't bear losing her child. So she tries to hold her child back, to keep him young and dependent.

When Parents Expect Perfection

Another kind of parent who is difficult for a child is the one who expects perfection. This parent doesn't do obviously abusive things to a child, and he doesn't neglect to feed, clothe or spend time with the child. But he takes the joy and hopefulness out of life by insisting that anything done imperfectly is not worth doing. He likely uses the same impossibly high standards for himself and his child.

This type of parent evaluates everything. He can't relax and enjoy the simple experiences of playing, eating or being in nature. Everything is measured. Everything is on a scale from worst to best. And only the best is worth anything. Good isn't good. Only perfect is good.

When a child has a parent who is a perfectionist, she is likely to feel tense a lot of the time. Even when away from the parent, the tension may persist because the parent's expectations of perfection accompany the child. Also, the child may not know that others don't have the same unreasonable expectations as her mom or her dad. This youth may have many experiences of shame, because she will feel she's falling short of her parent's expectations, which soon become her own expectations. She may give others a break and show some tolerance for them, but she's less likely to give herself a break. She can't figure out how to love herself, or to feel lovable to others, unless she's perfect. And she knows–though may not admit it–that she *can't* be perfect. So life becomes an exhausting, losing battle.

If a boy has a perfectionist mom and he tries to protest to his mother about her expectations, she likely will sit him down and explain to him the importance and legitimacy of her high standards. She is not going to see that she's demoralizing and damaging her child. She will insist she's teaching him how to succeed in this competitive world. She may leave him feeling ashamed of his complaints because she is so sure of herself. She is sure that she is right and so he must be wrong to question her. He'll feel ashamed that he's trying to take "the easy way" (his mother's words) and is not tough enough to strive and struggle to do things "correctly."

This child needs a dog. I'm joking a little bit here, but my point is that dogs don't evaluate whether things or people are perfect. They just enjoy what feels good in the moment and go looking for the next good thing. People aren't dogs and they do have to do some planning and evaluating and at times they'll want or need to work hard and reach high, but we can learn a lot about joy and affection from animals. The perfectionist parent wouldn't appreciate these comments much. He or she would think they are frivolous and silly and might lead a child to stray from the serious business of becoming a successful adult. But what is success in life really? Some might say that enjoying and appreciating yourself and others while engaging in interesting and satisfying activities makes for a successful life, even if others are making more money or getting more awards.

Depending on the child's own nature and on his abilities and temperament, the child of a perfectionist may go the route of becoming a perfectionist herself. If the parent's perfectionism isn't too extreme and it's not conveyed with pessimism about the child's prospects, a child may be able to identify with the parent and may have a reasonably happy life working to reach very high standards. If she has children, she will expect the same of them.

Perfectionism suits some temperaments better than others. So a perfectionistic parent may be a bigger burden to one child than to another. If a parent's perfectionism clashes greatly with a child's temperament or his abilities, the young person may rebel, either actively or passively. An actively rebellious youth might leave school to pursue a dream to travel the world, or he might relocate to Los Angeles to become a street musician. He will choose a course that's very different from anything his parent would endorse and openly pursue it.

A more passive approach to rebellion might be to get lazy about school, to oversleep and lose homework papers, and start to fail in school for reasons the child can't identify. Falling into depression or getting heavily into smoking pot might also represent more passive ways to rebel against a parent's oppressive perfectionism.

A parent with high standards is not necessarily a perfectionist parent. High standards can be good for young people if they are within reach of the child's actual abilities and if they are presented in an optimistic and encouraging way as great goals for which to strive. They are not absolute necessities the child has got to reach in order to avoid worthlessness and to retain a parent's love. If high standards are part of a belief system that states that effort brings meaning to life and is to be applauded, they can serve kids well, especially if hard work is not the *only* thing valued within the family. Parents who know how to have fun and relax in an unpressured atmosphere will likely be successful in encouraging kids that there's a time for play and also a time for committed effort.

The Immature Parent

The immature parent is the perfectionist parent's opposite. Instead of expecting too much from herself and from you, she expects very little. Expectations and thoughts of the future aren't of much importance to her.

Immature parents generally aren't mean or abusive, and they take care of the basics such as food and shelter, but their immature behavior makes them unreliable for their kids. I'm thinking of parents who don't fully understand the normal role of a parent, which is to be aware of the present and future needs of their kids and to be active in trying to assure those needs are met. Good parents act as scouts who watch the road ahead. They make sure the obstacles aren't too great and make sure their kids are equipped for the challenges that lie ahead. They don't just wander down the road with their child, as a buddy might, and see what happens. They're a bit more planful and aware than that. In contrast, the immature parent is childlike. He's often engaged in doing what's fun for him and he may forget to consider his child. Or he may try to consider his child, but he doesn't quite know how because he doesn't have a good sense of who his child is and what his child needs, now or in the future. Like a child himself, he may try for a while, but get discouraged easily and give up. Or his feelings get hurt and he retreats to his room to play video games, or goes out golfing or drinking without any thought of others in the family. An immature parent can be lots of fun at times. Your friends might think you're lucky because your mom doesn't set a curfew or even know that you're out late, and she's fun to party with; maybe she lets you and your friends share her stash of pot. But *you* likely won't think you're lucky, because you don't feel like your mom really has your back. Sure, she can be fun, and it's kind of nice that she doesn't nag you about getting homework and chores done, but you feel unsettled by the fact that she doesn't know what's going on in your life and isn't thinking about your future. You're not sure who is going to help you with the more serious challenges of growing up. Yeah, she's great at a party, she's funny and free-wheeling, but that's what friends are for. And not everything in your life is a party.

If you have an immature parent, you may find it hard to get angry at her. After all, she's not actively hurting you, and your friends say she's a trip. But you probably will be angry with her, because she's not doing what parents ought to. She's not helping you along the road toward adulthood. She's leaving you too much on your own. She may even encourage some behaviors that aren't good for you in the long run, for example, staying up too late on school nights, experimenting with marijuana, gambling, early sex, or living totally in the moment while ignoring planning and responsibility. You may know (and resent) that this approach to life isn't going to get you into a good college or prepare you for adulthood.

As hard as it can be for a teenager to be seen in public with old-fashioned, uncool, predictable parents, being with an immature parent is often worse. An immature parent may embarrass a child. He may put personal things on his Facebook page and add some of his teenaged child's friends as Facebook friends, which means that his child's friends will see Dad's dumb behavior. Or he may come to a school assembly in beach clothes or party clothes because he is all about fun and making a splash and he isn't thinking about how his kid will feel when he makes himself the center of attention in these ways.

A child of an immature parent may go the route of becoming pals with that parent. At least that keeps the two of them sort of close and they can have some fun together. Becoming buddies doesn't mean the child isn't feeling anger or stress. It just means that the child is trying to find something good in the less-than-ideal situation. Another coping strategy is for the child of an immature parent to become hyper-responsible. He becomes everything his parent isn't: organized, disciplined, concerned, considerate and attentive. These developments are certainly not all bad and may lead to a very productive adult life, but they can be signs of a child under a lot of pressure to provide for himself what a parent can't provide. And since a child isn't an adult and isn't really ready for so much responsibility, there's usually a lot of anxiety mixed in with his efforts. He'll have trouble relaxing because everything depends on him and can easily fall apart. He may develop an anxious and driven personality that will make it hard for him to enjoy himself and to allow those around him to relax. He would be better off if he could bring some reliable adults into his life—perhaps a coach, youth group leader, or friend's parent—so he can lean on them a bit and get some good guidance and support.

Chapter 8

POWERHOUSE FEELINGS

I'd like to take a closer look at some of the emotions kids of troubled parents may feel. You may have these feelings whether you have a troubled parent or not, but if you have a parent with problems, chances are you may have an especially tough struggle with some or all of these "powerhouse feeling." Which of these emotions is hardest for you probably depends on what kind of parenting problems your parent has and whether your parent's problems mainly make her sad and sickly, mean and abusive, or irresponsible. It also depends on your unique personality and on other factors in your life, like the age you were when things got tough and the presence or absence of other people there to support you. I should add that I am not covering all the difficult feelings people can have, just a sampling of them.

GUILT

We've already talked some about guilt. Guilt is one of several powerhouse feelings kids with troubled parents may confront. You are especially likely to struggle with guilt if your parent has a lot of pain, seems helpless to function normally, or if he does out-of-control things (such as driving drunk) that cause him or other people serious problems. People often struggle with guilt when those they care about are getting hurt.

Guilt occurs when you think maybe you caused the hurt or you failed to prevent it when you could have. Usually guilt is a nagging feeling inside that says you should have done this or that or you shouldn't have done this or that; you tell yourself that if you had done more, or done differently, or refrained from doing what you did, maybe no one would have gotten hurt.

Sometimes people hide from their guilty feelings because the feelings are painful. But you may see clues that a person has a guilt-problem if he keeps doing things to hurt himself; his behavior suggests he has a guilty conscience that's telling him he needs to be punished. A young man might get into accidents or lose his homework over and over or sleep late on a test day so he has to finish his exam in half the allotted time. He makes sure bad things happen to him, which suggests he isn't feeling entitled to good things. Guilty people may feel overwhelming urges to cut themselves or may be unable to relax and enjoy life because they don't feel entitled to pleasure.

Sometimes people ask, "What's wrong with guilt? Aren't you supposed to feel guilty some of the time?" Nothing is wrong with guilt and, yes, you are supposed to feel guilty some of the time. But the time to feel guilty is when you really have hurt someone else, perhaps out of carelessness, meanness, or childishness. Then it's appropriate to feel guilty for a while and to use that guilt as a signal that you need to re-think your behavior and perhaps change it in the future. If you use guilt in that way, guilt is serving a good purpose.

But it's not useful to feel guilty about things that aren't your responsibility and aren't under your control. So it's not of any value to feel guilty that you had fun swimming at the lake while your mother was hospitalized due to her schizophrenia. And it's not sensible to feel guilty because your father gambled away his paycheck and couldn't pay for a birthday present for your younger brother. Feeling guilty about those things suggests you have power over things you don't.

I've already talked about how tempting it can be to believe you're powerful in a situation in which you're really not, but pretending to have that kind of power causes problems later in life. So it's better to say "no" to unreasonable responsibility and guilt whenever you can. In those situations in which you've really done something wrong, you can use your guilt as a sign it's time to straighten up your act. Then let the guilt go; it's done its job. If you hold onto guilt after it's done its job, it becomes a burden you carry that keeps you from using your positive energy. If you carry a hammer to work because you need it to build a staircase, but after the staircase is built you take the heavy hammer with you when you go for a swim in the lake, how smart is that?

RAGE

We've talked some about the rage kids feel when parents deliberately hurt them. Let's take that discussion further. If your parent injures you through physical mistreatment or emotional mistreatment, you are likely to feel great anger. The anger comes primarily from the idea that someone who should care for you and protect you chooses instead to harm you and to deprive you of the basic rights all human beings should have. So you feel rage and also something called outrage, which is an indignant feeling that says, "How dare you do that to me? What right do you have?" Outrage is about standing up for what you're entitled to, or standing up for the rights of another person who is being abused. It's about making a judgment that says, "This treatment of me (or my brother, friend, or community) is wrong."

Even if your parent hurts you without clearly intending to, you likely will feel anger. Young people have an expectation that parents will protect them, not harm them. Say for example your mother abuses drugs when she gets depressed. When she takes too many pills, she gets sleepy and confused and out of it. If she's promised to take you shopping for school clothes, the promise gets forgotten. Her behavior is so weird and unpredictable, you're afraid to bring kids to your house. She's not abusing drugs deliberately to hurt you, but she's also not refraining from her destructive behavior in order to be a responsible parent. You have reason to be angry because your needs and rights have been neglected.

Here is another example, of a different type. Imagine your mother and father have lost a newborn baby and they're very depressed for a long, long time. They have a reason to be sad and they actually may be unable to take an interest in your schoolwork, friends, and summer plans. Even if you understand the loss they have suffered and you want to be patient with them, you *still* may feel angry at them and wish things were different. Anger isn't always reasonable. It doesn't go away just because you know your parent "can't help it." So give yourself a break and don't get down on yourself for being mad. It's just what you feel. You can't help it any more than your parents can help being sad if they've lost a baby. You and your parents are different people in different situations. Each of you has the feelings that make sense for your age and your circumstances. You may want to refrain from yelling and screaming at your parents since you understand their situation, but it's all right to feel angry inside.

Sometimes people try to escape from their anger. A person may find anger tiring or find that it leaves her feeling like a bad person. Anger is especially hard to bear if your parent triggers the anger by mistreating you, then he condemns you as a bad person because you're angry. Unfortunately, lots of emotionally abusive parents do just that. If our anger is held up to us by others as "proof" that we're no good, then our anger loses much of its power to help us feel stronger. Our anger becomes our enemy, which is too bad because anger in some situations makes a lot of sense and, in moderation, can bring a healthy feeling of strength. Another thing that can happen is that our anger fails to change the people we want it to influence. We feel like we're beating our head against a wall. We feel tired out and don't feel at all powerful. For all these reasons and others, people sometimes try to hide from their anger.

One way to hide from anger is to change it into another experience that doesn't look like anger. We saw how guilt sometimes shows up as self-punishing behavior, such as getting into accidents or failing in school. Anger can show up under a few disguises too. If you can spot those disguises, that knowledge can help you a great deal because you'll recognize the cloaks for anger and you'll be able to see your anger and deal with it more directly. Here are a few ways people hide from anger:

Some people handle their anger by going numb. They feel foggy or distant at times. They're not quite "all there." At times of stress, they may suddenly feel unreal or they feel like the people around them aren't real. These unreal feelings hide a person's very real anger. They can hide other difficult feelings (such as shame and fear, even excitement) as well.

Some people avoid anger by getting depressed. They feel that life sucks, there's nothing good in the whole world. They can't imagine why anyone would want to be alive. They hope they'll get in an accident and die young.

These two ways of handling anger have something in common. They involve being slowed down, passive, and low-energy. They involve withdrawing from life. They work as disguises for anger because they don't look or feel anything like anger, which is hot, energetic, and engaged. They are ways to turn off anger so you don't have to deal with the discomfort it brings.

Another disguise for anger is to express it indirectly, so it doesn't look a lot like ordinary anger. For example, you may show your negative feelings for a friend not by telling her directly that you're angry but by finding a way to make her life hard. You might lose some class notes she loaned you or accidentally dent the new bike that's giving her pleasure. Or you may just forget to call her back whenever she calls you. Psychologists describe this way of acting as *passive-aggressive*. The difference between direct aggression and passive aggression is the difference between (a) picking up a rock and throwing it at someone you're mad at and (b) just happening to drop a rock in the person's path so she'll trip when she gets to it. Passive-aggression isn't really all that passive. It just looks that way. Instead of telling your mother you're furious that she's going out on another date with a man who made a pass at you, you drive her car until it runs out of gas and you forget to tell her it's stranded down the road. That's not so passive, is it? It's just not taking responsibility for your wishes and feelings.

Another way to disguise anger is by doing something called "identification with the aggressor." That means you start acting like the person who's hurting and angering you. If your father blows up at you and knocks you around and insults you, you start doing that same thing to your younger brother or to a little kid on the school playground. You feel better because now you're the tough guy, not the one picked on. You feel powerful and in control, not small and helpless. The problem with this anger-disguise is that you're choosing to act like someone you don't like or respect, which means in the end you won't like or respect yourself. You may also hurt innocent people, just as you were hurt.

Some people hide from anger and other feelings by becoming mechanical. They act and feel as if they are computers or machines, not flesh and blood people. They live life by strict rules and procedures and try to forget about feelings. They lose their sense of humor. These changes make it hard for them to socialize with other people.

The best way to handle anger is to admit you're angry, then try to understand why you're angry without getting down on yourself about your feelings. If you are being mistreated, do whatever you can to stop the mistreatment, while at the same time realizing that your power may be limited.

We've talked about anger being natural when you're hurt. You get angry as a way to protest and to protect yourself. Your anger says, Stop, don't do this to me, I've done nothing to deserve this pain. You hope your anger will be a strong message to the person who's hurting you, a message that tells him to stop. Unfortunately though, abusive parents often don't get the message. Sometimes they even get-off on your distress and anger, so they step up the abuse. Either way, the abuse continues and your anger continues. Your anger may start to feel like a burden, not a useful tool.

If your anger isn't helping, if it's just leaving you tired and discouraged and you're starting to disguise it in one of the ways we've discussed, it's time to think about whether there's a way to let go of it. You may be able to find an honest way to think about your situation that lets you put down at least a part of your anger. For example, you have a mentally ill parent who promises to take you places you're longing to go and never carries through. You may be able to say to yourself, Okay, I have a right to be angry about missing out on some things, but this anger's getting me nowhere. I'm going to stop expecting much from Mom. I won't set myself up for anger and disappointment by falling for all the big plans and promises. Instead, I'm joining the Outings Club at school. I know I can count on the club leaders to follow through.

It can actually be scary to let go of anger because it can mean letting go of some deep wishes, such as the wish for a reliable mother. When you let go of your anger, you're saying to yourself, "My protest is *never* going to get me a healthy mother." Even though that's an upsetting idea to accept, you may feel better letting go of your wish if you know you're just beating your head against the wall trying to get it met. Once you've let the wish go, you can put your energy into getting some good mothering from other adults instead of from a mother who can't give it.

If you currently are being badly victimized, for example, by sexual or physical abuse, you will not be able to let go of anger. You should do anything in your power to get help for your situation from a trusted adult. After you get relief from the abuse, then you can work on getting past your anger if your anger burdens you.

Kids who have been badly victimized sometimes get angry at odd times, perhaps over seemingly little things. Sometimes you don't know why you're angry and you may feel you can't control the feeling. It may be you're angry because some little thing in the present is reminding you of something awful done to you in the past, but you don't quite make the connection—you just all of a sudden feel frighteningly irritable or furious. It may help you to know that your reaction isn't unusual for people who have been abused. Your anger isn't crazy or irrational. There's a logic to it that you just can't see at the moment.

Figuring out what you're really angry about can help you feel more in control. It can also help you to let go of your anger, if you want to do that. You may be able to figure things out by stopping to think about your feelings. Be forewarned though that it's sometimes hard to figure out where our strong feelings come from and why they stay with us. If you want to understand more about your anger but you can't get there on your own, you may want to get some adult, professional help. A therapist may be of great value to you in helping you better understand your anger and other feelings.

SHAME

Shame is another feeling that often plagues kids whose parents have problems. Shame means you feel bad about who you are. You think you don't measure up to others. You think you're not much of a person, that others are better than you. Shame is a feeling people can have at any age but teens are especially vulnerable to shame, even if they don't have troubled parents to complicate their lives. Any time you're trying to manage a new situation and you're worried about whether you're going to manage it well, you're vulnerable to shame. Being a teen is all about managing what's new (such as developing an adult body and mind and meeting all the challenges that go with that), so all teens are likely to have experiences of shame.

Let's think about why having a troubled parent might bring feelings of shame. I can think of a few reasons. Sometimes kids take a parent's problem as a personal failure, and personal failures often bring shame. Kids can have the idea that a better kid would be able to fix her parent's problems. A better kid would cheer up a depressed father, or calm a worried mother, or convince a paranoid mother that the CIA is not out to get her, or persuade a father with a dangerous habit to give it up. Not true! Kids very seldom can fix adults' emotional problems. No matter how smart, funny, goodhearted, or patient a person you are, that's still going to be the case. So try not to put yourself down for not fixing your parent's problems when it's not reasonable to expect yourself to do so.

Another idea that bothers some kids is the idea that a better kid naturally would have gotten a better parent, that is, a parent who is healthy, nice, reliable, and even-tempered. You have a feeling that a truly good kid wouldn't get assigned a not-so-terrific parent in the great parent lottery, as if fate or nature or God gives great parents to all great kids. Again, not true. Your parents are not a reflection on you.

You and your parents are separate people. No matter how troubled they may be or how embarrassing their behavior, that doesn't make you any less a person. You may have had bad luck in the parent department. That happens. It's not your fault and it doesn't make you any less valuable than your friend or schoolmate who's got an award-winning parent. So hold your head up. Lots of successful, smart, good people had lousy or troubled parents. When you come to admire an actress, a rock star, or a senator, you don't worry about what kind of parents that person had. You judge the person on his own qualities. When you meet a jerky, dishonest, mean kid at school, you don't say, "Her mom's nice so she must be nice too." You say, "Even though her mom's nice, she isn't."

Where do kids get the idea that they are bound to be just like their parents? In part it comes from early childhood wishes to be exactly like Mom or Dad. Very young children often feel they don't have many strengths or skills of their own. They look around and see that most people are bigger and more capable than they are. They don't want to feel small and inept, so they "borrow" strengths from the people closest to them, usually their parents or older brothers and sisters. They say, "My dad is big" (so I don't have to feel little) or "My mom can drive a car" (so it's okay that I can't). They compare their parents with other kids' parents because they're borrowing their parent's strengths and thinking, "If my mom is smarter, then I'm smarter."

It's also true that young children are very dependent on parents, and parents are very involved with the young child, so it's natural for the child to feel that she and her parent are a unit. The self extends to include the other. The *we* is as important as the *I*. In that environment, identification with the parent is so natural that the parent's strengths become one's own, as do the parent's shortcomings.

When you're older, you don't need to do so much sharing with and borrowing from your parent, because you've developed your own size, strength, personality, and abilities. But the idea of getting your worth from your parents' worth may still be with you. If you like what you see in your parents, that idea doesn't do you much harm; in fact, it can help you feel secure. But if you don't think highly of your parents, the tie that likely started out as a boost to your self-esteem becomes a drag on your confidence.

If that's what's happening, it's time to inform yourself that your value doesn't come from your parents. In fact, it never did, even when you were three years old. It never was true that your mom being smart made you smart or your dad being strong made you strong. You didn't really have their strengths then and you don't have to feel dragged down by their weaknesses now. Another thing you can do for yourself is to make attachments to people and groups you can feel proud of. Make sure though, when you do that, that the group you join really stands for what you value and respect. Don't join a violent gang just to belong to a group. That's no better than staying identified with a parent you don't respect.

I said in the last paragraph that older people don't need to borrow strength from the people around them in the way little kids do. As a teenager though, you're still developing and much in life is new to you, so you may not feel strong and accomplished a lot of the time. Your self-esteem feels shaky and that leaves you sensitive about the people with whom you're associated, as if their qualities will rub off on you. Teenagers often feel ashamed to be associated with people they don't think highly of, or people they think could be teased by others. You may go way out of your way not to be seen with someone you think is physically unattractive or socially awkward. You may feel that if you're seen with someone, then whatever is shameful or vulnerable about him or her will carry over to you and you'll be unattractive in other people's eyes, maybe even in your own eyes, which will feel awful. Teenagers often don't like to be seen with their parents for these same reasons, even if their parents are good people. All the uncool things about your parents seem to stick out like so many sore thumbs when your friends are around, and you think people will associate those things with you. You may also feel as if your continued dependency on your parents will be visible and shameful, even though it's entirely normal.

The problem of shame is even worse when you have a mentally ill, alcoholic, or abusive parent. The sense that what they've got carries over to you can be very upsetting. As you get older, you will begin to see that you remain yourself no matter what company you are in. Other people's negative traits don't rub off on you. And your peers probably won't get you confused with the unkempt person beside you just because the two of you are standing side by side, or with your parent because you have genes in common. If they do, your friends have some growing up to do.

Some kids of troubled parents worry about becoming more and more like a disturbed parent as the child gets closer to adulthood. That view of your future is another cause for feeling ashamed and worried about who you are. But it's not necessary to be like your parents if you don't want to be. No one is fated to turn out a certain way. It's not true that if your parent is abusive, you'll necessarily abuse your children, or that depressed parents always have depressed children. Put your energy into figuring out what kind of person you'd like to become and working to become that person.

If you keep noticing that you try to be one way, but you "turn out" another way you don't like, take a good look at your own behavior. Probably you're doing some things you may not have noticed to get yourself off track. For example, say your father was a poor student and grew up to be an irresponsible business executive who made lots of bad business deals and escaped his problems by drinking. You've decided to be a good student whose future will be different from your father's. You keep starting out well with your classes, but late in the term something always goes wrong and you do badly on your finals and get lousy grades. Don't just slip into shame and depression about being destined to be like your dad. Think about what you're *doing* to end up that way.

Probably you're slacking off near the end of the term on purpose (though maybe you haven't admitted that to yourself). Probably you've got some reasons for doing it, for instance, you might be scared that if you outshine your dad he'll get more depressed, or maybe he'll get angry with you, or won't feel close to you. In other words, maybe you're afraid to do well, which is very different from being fated to be like your dad. If you think hard about your behavior and you still feel stuck in the same bad pattern, it's time to get some adult help.

Some kids of troubled parents worry that they've inherited whatever it is that makes their parent messed up. They feel that if something bad has come to them through their genes, there's no escaping it. It's true that some traits are inherited and can't be avoided. Mostly those traits are things like eye color and height that don't have anything to do with how worthwhile or capable a person you are. If your parent has a mental illness and you're worried about inheriting that, try not to torment yourself with such a worry. The evidence about inheritance of mental illness is not that strong. It may be true that some people are more susceptible to certain kinds of difficulties than others. That doesn't mean you're going to get the problem or that you're powerless to help yourself if you're more susceptible than the next person. Nourishing your personal strengths is the best protection against mental illness or addiction, so try to put your energy into developing and enjoying your strengths, not worrying about future illness. If you think you are developing symptoms of a mental illness or addiction, you should talk to a trusted adult and possibly visit a doctor. That's a good idea whether or not you have mental illness or addiction in your family.

Kids who are concerned about becoming like troubled parents sometimes go overboard worrying about every little similarity between themselves and their parents. They feel that it's not safe to have any qualities of their parent's. They try to be their parent's opposite, even where that's not necessary. They panic if they see any similarity at all between themselves and their parent and they waste energy trying to get rid of it.

If it's your father's meanness you don't like, then try not to be mean in the way your father is, but don't get bent out of shape about having your father's sense of humor or his red hair or his way of telling stories. Those things aren't problems. In fact, they may be good things (or at least neutral things) you can feel free to share with your parent. Sharing those parts of a parent doesn't mean you'll one day share his meanness, his depression, or his alcoholism.

Also, you don't have to go to the opposite extreme to be different from your parent. If your mother is too hard-hearted, you don't have to be the most tender-hearted person in the whole world. If your father is promiscuous, you don't have to be completely asexual. You can be in the middle of the road and still be free of your parent's problem.

I can't cover all the reasons kids of troubled parents sometimes feel ashamed, because there are many of them and they vary with a person's situation. For example, a teenage boy who is beat up by his father may feel ashamed for "taking it." He feels as if a tougher, better kid wouldn't let his father get away with that abuse. But a second teenage boy, who fights back against his father and leaves his father bruised and upset, feels ashamed for hurting his father. He thinks, "What kind of person would beat up his own dad? I must be a freak." These two examples may give you an idea of how hard it can be for an abused child to avoid shame. Often, there's no way to cope with an abuse situation that doesn't bring some shame.

Some abused kids try to fend off shame by becoming "shameless." That means that a person tells himself that everything he does is cool, that anything goes, that nothing's against his own inner code of behavior or is cause for shame (or guilt). *If I beat up my dad, no sweat. If I let him beat me, what's the big deal?* If nothing matters or is good or bad, then there's no reason for shame. Shamelessness is not a great solution to the shame problem because it leaves a person without values, and values guide us throughout life and give our lives meaning. They also help us to build strong relationships. A better solution is to try to avoid unnecessary shame by looking at situations realistically. And when shame does come—as it does for everyone at times—try to comfort yourself and let the shame pass so you can get back to enjoying life.

GRIEF

All kids of troubled parents have cause for grief. That's true whether your parent is abusive, psychotic, alcoholic, or depressed (or troubled in some other way). Grief is the deep sadness that comes when you have to accept that certain things you wished for will never come to pass, or when you have to accept that good things that once were yours have been lost. Grief comes after deaths, but with other losses as well. It is a normal part of every life, but some kids deal with more grief or earlier grief than others.

The grief that comes from having a parent whose troubles keep them from really *being* a parent can be very deep. One of the important experiences of childhood and adolescence is the experience of being loved and supported by parents (and of returning that love).

Realizing that a parent cannot love you or cannot take care of you due to his or her troubles can bring a painful sadness, in addition to other feelings such as anger and helplessness. Sometimes the sadness and helplessness are so powerful that kids go to great lengths to get away from the feelings. They may say they're not like others; they don't care about having loving parents. They don't care about love and affection period. They don't even care about or have feelings of any kind. Or a child may pretend her parents love her deeply and look after her well, even though it's obvious that those things simply aren't true. Kids pretend true things are untrue when they fear they may not be able to bear the truth.

Having an unloving, uncaring parent is a tough truth to bear. In the long run though, it's best to try to stand up to it. Then you can begin to sort out the meaning of that truth. For example, it doesn't mean there's anything wrong with *you*. It doesn't mean you're not a good or lovable person and it absolutely does not mean that no one will love you in the future; it just means you've been unlucky in that you were born to an unloving parent.

It's especially hard in adolescence to mourn the fact that you had a deeply disappointing parent. Adolescence is the time of life in which all children, of all parents, move away from day to day closeness with parents and move on to day to day closeness with people their own age. So even if you've had loving parents, you are facing a scary process of letting go of your childhood ties. The scariness of this letting-go is especially great if you feel you never got what you needed from your parents. Now you must face that you never will get that love, support, and guidance from your parents. That idea can feel overwhelming, so that you want to push it away and pretend it isn't true. But hard as this job is, if you have the courage to feel the sadness and regret over having a disappointing parent who never will be able to go back and undo the hurts he inflicted on you, you'll be better off for it. You'll be able to look at the unmet needs you may have and think about who, other than your parents, might help you meet them. Perhaps you will look to friends' parents, or to a minister, coach, or therapist. You also may work hard to make good friendships with reliable, caring peers who can give you some of what your parents can't give.

Chapter 9

TROUBLED PARENTS AND ORDINARY TEEN LIFE

Healthy parents help their teens with the challenges of growing up. Troubled parents unfortunately can make adolescence more difficult and confusing than it needs to be. Rather than easing their kids' inner struggles over tasks such as leaving home and coming of age sexually, troubled parents intensify those struggles. Let's look at some of the big issues for young people and consider how troubled parents may hurt rather than help.

SEPARATION FROM HOME AND PARENTS

It's natural for older children and teenagers to get more and more interested in people their own age. As a teenager, your world becomes larger and you're less focused on what's going on at home. That doesn't mean your family is no longer important to you; it just means you're preparing to be an adult who likely will find a partner or companions your own age and will not live with your parents.

Healthy parents may feel some sadness and may worry about their children as they move out into the world, but they will also see the positive side of their children's increased independence. They will know that independence is crucial for their children's future happiness, so they will support their kids' efforts to explore the world, make friends, and develop interests and skills. They may rein a child in from time to time if the child is going too fast or is trying things that are unsafe or require more experience than the young person has, but overall, they'll encourage their kids' independence. When a child is feeling fearful about independence, a good parent will be there to encourage him or to give suggestions about how to manage new situations.

Troubled parents often discourage kids' independence and make kids feel bad about their interests in the world outside the family. Some troubled parents discourage their kids by exaggerating the dangers of the outside world so that their kids feel more than normally afraid to try new things. "That will never work," your father might say, or "Don't go, you'll get in an accident and be texting me to come get you," or "When your older brother started dating as much as you're doing now, he got mononucleosis and had to be in bed for six months."

Some troubled parents dramatize how much they will miss their child and how sad and lonely they will feel when the child is away. They may even suggest that something bad is likely to happen to them when the child is far from home. "I hope I don't get sick while you're out living your carefree life," your mother might say or, "I hope I can keep this old stove from blowing up while you're off with your Facebook friends." While you're out you may find yourself wondering and worrying about your parent instead of paying attention to what you're doing.

Other troubled parents may demean your activities, so you're encouraged to feel they're not worth pursuing. "You're going to *that* movie? It's such junk," your father says or, "Why do you even bother going out with those kids? They seem like a bunch of nitwits" or, "If that's the kind of schoolwork you're doing, good luck in college."

Some parents directly guilt-trip their kids about their healthy preference to be with peers. "I suppose you'd rather be out with those friends of yours than stay home with me and Dad." "Now that you can drive and get around without me, I guess you can take me for granted. I'm just your mother after all." Other troubled parents heighten their kids' anxiety by hinting that they may abandon a child if he gets too independent. A father might say, "You don't need me anymore. I might as well just move to Hawaii, I've always wanted to live there. I stayed in the frozen Midwest only for you kids." Or, "If you're grown up enough to date that Mary, you might as well get a job and move out on your own."

If your parent responds to your increasing independence like any of the parents above, then your parent is having a problem letting you grow up. It's scary to think your parent might abandon you or be angry with you for wanting to reach out into the world in a way that's healthy and normal. It's especially hard to bear your parents' comments about the dangers of independence if you've got your own worries about independence, as most kids do. But try not to let your parent keep you from doing what's best for you, and try not to use your parent's negative attitude as an excuse to flee from situations that are scary for you but worth confronting.

For example, say you're frightened to ask a girl to a dance but you know it would be a good thing to do, and you know if she says "yes" you'll feel great you did it. Your mother notices you're nervous and instead of giving you support she starts teasing you: "Scared to ask that girl out, aren't you? Do you think she's finally noticed she's a head taller than you?" Part of you wants to blow up and say, "Just forget it. I won't go to the stupid dance." But if you do that, you're just hurting yourself. So try to stick to your task even though your mother is making it harder for you.

COMPETENCE

During your later childhood and teen years, you have the potential to develop many new areas of competence that will ready you for adult life. Your mind develops new powers of reasoning and understanding. Your body has more strength and agility. You may develop your own special sense of humor, as well as creativity and the ability to empathize with others. Competent, healthy parents want to see their children develop their abilities. They take pleasure in their children's strengths. Troubled parents may discourage competence in their children.

A child's competence may be threatening to a troubled parent. Some troubled parents feel overly competitive with their children. A father may feel that his son's new muscle strength makes the father's body seem puny; he may feel that his authority in the family is suddenly in doubt. That father may belittle his son, saying, "You think that mountain you climbed was a big deal, but you didn't even need ropes or pitons. You should have seen the peak I climbed when I was your age." The father may hope this belittling will subdue his son's pride in his abilities and keep the boy under the father's thumb.

Another troubled parent may feel that she can't relate to or feel close to a competent daughter, since she herself is not an accomplished person. She may whine to her daughter about the daughter's abilities, saying, "You'll grow up and get a great job in New York or Paris. I'll be left here, while you're out doing all those things I never could do. I would have been better off with a normal daughter, who wasn't such a brain." Insecure parents can feel especially threatened and excluded when their kids have areas of competence that are alien to the parent, for example, advanced computer skills.

Another type of parent might suggest that his child's new abilities are like destructive weapons that the child will one day use against others. A father might say, "You're getting to be such a math whiz. You'll probably screw your brother out of his inheritance when the time comes." Or he might say, "You're becoming so ripped; I'd better watch my step or you'll be knocking me around." When a parent portrays a child's abilities as destructive or as likely to bring painful envy or depression to the parent, the child is discouraged from taking pride and pleasure in his abilities. He gets a persuasive message that his parent would be more comfortable if he stopped developing his abilities. Clearly, it's not in your best interest to stop developing your talents, and in the long run you can't protect your parent from low self-esteem by keeping your own capabilities under-developed and your self-esteem low.

SEXUAL DEVELOPMENT

One of the normal parts of being an adolescent is the growth of sexual feelings and fantasy. Kids often feel anxiety about sexual feelings since those feelings suddenly may be taking a new and often intense form and are associated with a mature body that is capable of acting on them, with significant consequences of pregnancy, disease, and altered feelings about self and others. Sexual feelings can bring great pleasure, but they also can bring worries about what feelings, fantasies, and behaviors are proper and normal and what ones aren't. And they can bring worries about whether one's wishes and body will be acceptable to others. Kids have to cope with a great many unsettling thoughts and questions. Is it okay to fantasize a lot? What about masturbation? Why do I have homosexual fantasies? Some of my fantasies seem weird; I bet no one else has them. I don't even understand what an orgasm is. My breasts aren't the same size. What if I get a disease? What if I get pregnant? What if I get a girl pregnant? What if I don't want to *ever* have sex? And on and on.

Healthy parents help their children to see that sexual feelings and thoughts are a normal and largely pleasurable part of being human. They also help their children sort out difficult questions about when to act on sexual feelings and when to hold back, what is safe and normal and what's a real cause for worry. They give this kind of help when it's needed and when kids are ready to accept it. They don't pry too much into personal feelings or have the expectation that their kids should share every private feeling or fantasy with a parent.

Troubled parents often make sexual development more difficult for their kids. Some troubled parents are threatened by their kids' sexual development, so they try to slow it down or stop it altogether by making the kids feel bad about their sexuality. These parents may make subtle or not so subtle comments suggesting that sexual interests are disgusting. "I suppose you're going out with that girl—*what's-her-name*—again," a mother says to her teenage son. "God only knows what the two of you do when you're alone."

Some parents are overly curious about their children's sexual life. They don't allow their children reasonable privacy, but have to be involved in everything and privy to everything. A mother might read a child's diary or snoop in his dresser drawers or constantly ask, "What were you two talking about? What were you doing out there in the car? What do you text about all day long?" The child gets the feeling he never can be alone with his peers or even with his private feelings and thoughts. His mother is always right there. If she's not present physically, she's in his thoughts because he knows he's in her thoughts.

Other troubled parents make sexual development difficult for their kids by setting bad examples. They manage their own sexual lives poorly, for example, by behaving promiscuously or talking too much about sex in ways that the child finds distasteful and immature. Such a parent may provoke her partner to anger, so that the child witnesses one parent enraged with the other over her sexual behavior. The child of such a parent may come to see sex as something out-of-control, immoral, or dangerous. Being sexual is no longer a private, pleasurable, adult experience. It's a public, provocative, unappealing thing that infuriates others.

Another parent may feel so possessive of a child that he can't allow the child her natural interest in people her own age. If a young woman is excited about a boy who's taken an interest in her, her jealous father may demean her interests as whorish, he may demean the boy she's interested in, or he may sabotage the teenagers' friendship by making rude or intimidating remarks to the boy when he telephones the house.

The more disturbed a parent, the more extreme may be his response to a child's normal sexual development. A parent who gets psychotic and has odd, delusional ideas may develop a crazy idea about his child's sexuality. For example, a father may become convinced that neighbors are using hidden cameras to spy on his daughter in her bedroom. Or he may believe that his daughter's sexual energy is causing his garden plants to die.

Some parents who have been sexually abusive of their younger-aged children will back off from sexual contact as the child matures, but their disturbed feelings for the young person may persist and express themselves in other destructive forms. For instance, a father may make harsh, crude, and demeaning comments portraying his daughter as a slut. The comments are a way to fend-off feelings about his *own* lack of sexual control, but they focus on the child in order to spare the father self-criticism. Other very disturbed parents may initiate sexual contact with a child once that child reaches puberty. A parent's insistence on a sexual relationship with a child is always wrong and is always deeply troubling to a young person and disturbing to his or her development.

If you have a troubled parent who is heightening your own natural anxieties about growing up and leaving home, about new abilities in school or sports, or about sexual development, it will help you to realize that your parent is adding to your anxiety unnecessarily due to problems of his or her own. Maybe you can find other sources of guidance and information. Make an effort to do that. Read books and think about whether the ideas in them make sense to you. Talk with trusted friends and with friends' parents if you can. Watch TV shows or read blogs shows about growing-up or go to talks at the library or community center. Not all the advice you get in these places will be right for you. You'll still have to sift through it and see what makes best sense, but try to expose yourself to views other than those of your parents so you won't think their ideas are the only ones in the world.

Chapter 10

SCAPEGOATING

We've talked about the value of recognizing when your parents, not you, are responsible for bad situations. That's a hard thing to do and an accomplishment if you can do it. There's another hard thing that's associated with that first one. Sometimes a young person with a troubled parent can get in the habit of blaming everything that goes wrong in his life on that parent. He goes overboard blaming his parent and stops looking honestly at who is responsible for what. If he doesn't study for a test and he fails it, he blames that on his parent. If he embarrasses a friend on Facebook, it's his parent's fault when he loses the friendship. If he gets a pimple and feels ugly, that's his parent's fault too.

This constant blaming is called scapegoating. A young person can be the victim of scapegoating (by parents or others) and he can do the scapegoating as well. At first glance, blaming everything on a disappointing parent might seem like a good solution to a kid's problems. He can get rid of a lot of bad feelings such as shame, self-disgust, and fear that way. And he can get rid of them by dumping them on someone who doesn't deserve a lot of sympathy anyway, since he's been a poor parent and has some responsibility, in an indirect way, for the child making poor choices in life. In the long run though, scapegoating is always a bad solution to uncomfortable feelings, no matter which person you use for your scapegoat, even if it's the devil himself.

One problem with scapegoating is that deep down you know you're blaming someone else for your own failings and you're likely to feel uncomfortable with that (as you should; the discomfort is a sign your conscience is working). Another problem is that you don't learn to take responsibility for your own shortcomings, which is something you need to do to become a reliable adult and to become a good parent yourself, should you choose to have children. Learning to take responsibility makes a person the kind of individual others can trust. In the long run, it makes you trust yourself more, too. If you're always covering up your mistakes, you get more and more afraid of those mistakes. You start to feel they can't be faced; they *have to be* covered up. You'll feel much more secure if you face up to your mistakes and realize they're not so awful. They're part of being human and you can try to do better next time.

As an example, think of Pedro who missed an important field goal at the end of a big football game. Pedro had been fantasizing for months about this game, each time imagining that he'd make a record-breaking kick at a crucial moment, and his teammates would carry him off the field on their shoulders with the crowd cheering wildly. Unfortunately, when the outcome of the game depended on Pedro's kick, he got a bad angle on the ball and his kick went left of the goal post. After the game, Pedro quietly started spreading rumors that the teammate who held the ball for the kick had held it improperly, so that Pedro had no shot at making a good kick. Deep down, Pedro knew he wasn't telling the truth. He felt ashamed of his lie and didn't feel much better about the missed kick.

If Pedro had taken responsibility for his poor performance, he wouldn't have ended up with the shame of dishonesty and cowardice. He also might have learned that our real performances can't always match our fantasies and that we, and our friends, can live with our less than perfect performances. His teammates would have forgiven him his poor kick and still liked him. By scapegoating someone else, he missed out on the chance to learn that it's okay to be imperfect.

Another problem with blaming someone else for all your shortcomings is that you get very dependent on that person. You start to feel you need her. She's like a garbage can you need for getting rid of all the not-so-great stuff inside you. You might get anxious if she's not around because suddenly you've got to take responsibility for your own garbage and you haven't learned how to do that. You may hang on to a relationship with the person you scapegoat even though you don't like her or enjoy her company. You keep her because she's your garbage can.

If you make your troubled parent your garbage can, you may end up sticking close to that parent long after you could have gotten out on your own and gotten away from the things you dislike about her. Or you might get away from your mother but look for a girlfriend you can use as a trash can, which will make for a bad relationship with that girl.

Abbas's mother was an alcoholic who had disappointed him throughout his life. When Abbas had trouble with his schoolwork in junior high school and then in high school, he got in the habit of blaming his mother for his failures. He'd say she gave him so many chores he couldn't do his work, or she wouldn't pay for the computer software he needed to get good grades, or she talked to him constantly and distracted him. When he went away to a junior college, he found a girlfriend who was a little bit talkative and distracting and he started blaming his bad grades and test scores on her. "If it weren't for Miriam," he'd say, "I'd be a straight A student." Miriam was the kind of girl who let Abbas get away with blaming her when she wasn't at fault. Abbas wasn't actually very fond of Miriam and he didn't respect her, but he felt nervous about breaking up with her. He half-realized that he'd come to depend on her as a scapegoat. He was afraid to be without her. If he didn't have Miriam, who would he blame for his bad grades?

Instead of finding a scapegoat, try to be honest about your own shortcomings and the things inside yourself that you don't like. Then give yourself some credit for being honest and don't be too hard on yourself about your faults. Try not to waste your energy beating yourself up about those faults or telling yourself everyone else is better than you (they're not). Just make efforts to do better over time; then you'll be pleased with yourself.

Chapter 11

TOO HIGH A PRICE TO PAY?– CHOOSING YOUR PARENT OVER YOURSELF

In a healthy family, you don't have to choose between being true to yourself and keeping your relationship with a parent. You can be true to your own needs and feelings without putting your relationship to your parent at risk. Your parent will be glad to see you respecting your own ideas and wishes.

This chapter is about those troubled families that force a child to choose between being true to himself and holding on to a relationship with a parent. I'll be talking about two different ways of being untrue to yourself. One kind of self-betrayal takes place mostly in the thoughts and feelings that you have about yourself. A second kind of self-betrayal takes place through your actions. Both ways of selling yourself out are efforts to hold on to a relationship with a parent by accepting wrong-headed ideas about yourself, especially ideas that portray your good qualities as bad qualities.

Kids may hold tight to relationships with parents even when the relationships are harmful. Some kids will twist themselves into human pretzels trying to let their parents off the hook for bad behavior, all in order to keep the tie with the parent. Often that pretzel-making in - volves having negative thoughts and feelings about yourself so you don't have to be angry with your parent.

Here's an example. Mary's mother died when Mary was five. Mary lives with her father. Her father is supposed to come home from work early one Saturday afternoon to take her to meet her friend Jan at the movies. It's a plan they've agreed upon, but Mary's father does-n't show up until it's too late to get to the movie. He offers the excuse that he got tied up with an important call. He doesn't apologize or make an alternate plan.

Unfortunately, this kind of thing has happened many times before, so Mary starts to feel irritated. But instead of saying to herself that she's angry with her dad and has a right to be, she faults herself for being selfish. She imagines other kids would be more appreciative of having a dad who has an important job and works so hard. She decides she's a rotten kid who is lucky to have such a good dad. Mary betrays herself in her feelings and thoughts.

Mary makes a plan to meet Jan for lunch on Sunday, since the Saturday plan fell through. She tells her father she's walking into town to meet Jan. He says, "I thought you'd be home to make my lunch." Mary explains she missed her date yesterday with Jan and doesn't feel she should cancel another plan. Her father says, "Well, do what you want, but I think you should reexamine your priorities. You might also think about who pays the bills around here." Mary starts to feel bad about herself again. She feels she's neglecting her father, which is what he wants her to feel. She calls and cancels her date with Jan. Here, Mary has betrayed herself in her feelings and in her actions too, because of her need to keep on good terms with her father.

It's not so hard to understand why kids sometimes choose to take on undeserved blame rather than hold a parent responsible for his own troubled behavior. Here are a few reasons I can think of:

You're afraid to face your disappointment in your parents because facing that disappointment brings a kind of separation. It means you lose some of your love and respect for a parent; you pull away from him inside, so in a sense you lose him. Think again of Mary, who has already lost her mother and might be very afraid of any kind of separation from her father.

You may also fear that your parent will pull away from you if he knows you're critical of him. He may abandon you, which is one of the scariest things there is. It's scary even during the teenage years be-cause you're already nervous then about growing up and being on your own. What if you lose your parent's support at that time? That's a hard thing to face.

Sometimes abandonment fear is a scary but groundless worry. In some families though, troubled parents do in fact reject children who refuse to lie to themselves about their parents' problems and refuse to take the blame for their parents' failings. Some parents pull away from these honest children.

A similar situation holds true for a child's fears of a parent's anger. Sometimes the fear is groundless, but sometimes there's a real danger. There are troubled parents who actually get very angry at their children when the children refuse to take the blame for the parent's failings, or when they confront the parent for his destructive behavior. Some parents get violently angry in a way that can be physically dangerous and can leave anyone close at hand feeling she may be blown off the face of the earth.

Let's look at what a young person can do to face up to fears of abandonment without wrongly taking blame on himself and hindering his own growth. One thing is to remind yourself that your parents are not the only people in the world who can support you as you grow and once you're an adult. In fact, if your parents are very troubled, they may be less able to give support than many other people are. You're paying too high a price if you're putting yourself down and coming to dislike yourself in order to keep your parent's support. It's not worth it. As you get older, you won't have to live with your parents but you will have to live with yourself. If you've had unsupportive, troubled parents you may be amazed to learn, later in life, how supportive other people can be to you. So even if you do lose your parents' backing, you don't need to be alone. Think about ways to reach out to other kids and other adults for support.

How can a child remain true to his own feelings and ideas if he thinks doing so may provoke anger in a parent? It's important to try to be realistic about your parent's temper. If your parent is a real threat to you physically, think twice about putting yourself in an unsafe situation by confronting him. You can stay true to your beliefs without saying them out loud and putting yourself in danger. If your father has a temper like Mount St. Helens, telling him off (even if he deserves it) is not a way to be good to yourself. If this is your situation, you need some help from other adults who can intervene with your parent and, if necessary, help you find a safer place to live. We'll talk more about that in Chapter 12.

If your parent's temper is scary and upsetting, but not physically dangerous, it may help to remind yourself that your parent isn't really as powerful as you might have thought when you were very little. No matter how big a temper she has, she can't split you apart just with the strength of her anger. Remember that her temper is her own problem. Try not to take it on as yours. Don't say, "Look how mad I made my mom" or, "She's so furious, I must have done something unforgivable." The reality is simply that she's mad and she has a horrid temper, that's all. You didn't *make* her mad, even if she says you did. Even if she's reacting to something you did, the reaction is hers; so if the reaction is unreasonable and out of control, that's her responsibility. Unfortunately, kids of disturbed parents often have to choose between being true to themselves and getting along with their parents. It's sad that this is true, but it's a fact of life for some kids. Another fact of life is that it never helps anything in the long run to sell yourself out, meaning to take blame that isn't yours or put yourself down when you don't deserve it. As much as you might want to keep on good terms with your parents as you grow up, it's more important to keep on good terms with yourself. If your relationship with your parents depends on your betraying yourself, the relationship isn't worth the price you're paying. It's better to make attachments to healthier, more grown-up people than to hold on to disturbed parents and lose yourself.

Chapter 12

POWER STRUGGLES

Power struggles aren't unique to troubled families. All families have them. Power struggles usually don't feel good, so why do we create them? Let's look at power struggles in general and then think about what those power struggles look like in families with a troubled parent.

Power struggles are about insisting our own will and wishes dominate or rule over someone else's. Often we get into these struggles when we're feeling a little insecure about how strong or capable we are and we want to show we're powerful by forcing someone else to accept our views or authority. A young person can feel as if taking advice or input from someone else means that something is wrong with her own idea; it isn't good enough on its own.

Let's take for an example Debbie who is asked by her mother to wash the dishes every Monday and Tuesday night. Debbie always gets the dishes washed, but she does it when she wants, according to her own schedule. She might wash the Monday dishes at midnight or wash them early Tuesday morning. Her mother has trouble understanding why she just doesn't wash them after dinner and get it over with and leave the family with a clean sink. But Debbie is stubborn about her right to wash the dishes whenever she chooses. She feels as if washing the dishes immediately after dinner is giving in to her mother. It's letting her mother run her life and letting her mother's will overpower hers. Washing the dishes late proves she's independent and strong-willed and not a little kid who's under her mother's thumb.

She and her mother sometimes fight about the dishes, with each one insisting her way is right. But since Debbie's mother is pretty mature, she backs off and gives Debbie a little space and doesn't get into a long, drawn-out power struggle with her. She tells her she'd like to see the dishes done after dinner and she wishes Debbie would think about whether she could get them done then, but if Debbie gets them done before the morning dishes get added to the pile, she'll settle for that.

As Debbie matures a little, she's able to see that her mother isn't dominating her or overpowering her by asking that the dishes be done earlier. She's also able to see that it's okay to do the dishes earlier to please her mother and that pleasing another person by cooperating with them doesn't make her a little kid. Compromising and working to please others are actually very adult things to do as long as you're not going against your own values or basic needs.

When you're resisting a sensible suggestion because you want to show you're grown up and have your own ideas, you can feel a little foolish inside. The more grown-up part of you may be thinking that it doesn't make sense not to cooperate with a reasonable request. Unfortunately, when we start to get that nagging foolish feeling inside, sometimes we get even more stubborn and press our point even harder. We do that because we're feeling a little weak and we want to get back to a strong feeling. If a young person's stubborn defense of his authority meets with a parent's equally stubborn defense of his authority, that makes for a power struggle in which coming out on top is more important than the issue being argued. Sound familiar? Most of us have been there.

Wise parents sometimes help kids not to get overly caught up in these struggles. They can say, "Do it when you're ready" without getting hung up about their own loss of authority. That helps a little because you don't feel forced into a corner in which complying means admitting you were wrong. A wise parent might also say, "I don't think what I'm asking is so unreasonable, so think about why you won't do it" (which encourages you to think for yourself). Or a parent might say, "Can't we find a way to work this out *together*," which reminds you that cooperation is possible and positive.

What happens in families with a troubled parent? Troubled parents can be provoked easily when kids make a big stand over a little issue. The parent can't take a step back and recognize that making big stands over small things can be a normal part of growing up and doesn't have to be taken as a serious threat to the parent's authority. You don't need to have a fight-to-the-death argument over it.

The troubled parent may feel overly threatened by the child's insistence on her point of view. A mother may feel she has to overpower her daughter, which only intensifies the conflict because the child needs her power to be recognized, not overwhelmed or negated. When the parent gets too invested in "showing who's right," that makes matters worse because the child finds it harder and harder to accept a parent's directions—no matter how reasonable—without feeling she's been defeated or humiliated. Another thing that can be difficult in families with troubled parents is that kids of troubled parents have gotten accustomed to their parent taking unreasonable positions, so when the parent takes a reasonable position, it can be hard to recognize and appreciate.

A way you can help yourself when you feel yourself getting into these painted-into-a-corner struggles is to step back and take a clear-eyed view at what was asked of you. If your brain says the request was reasonable, then respect your own good judgment and say to yourself, "It's okay to do what's been asked of me; it was a reasonable request and it's okay to say yes to it." If the request is really unreasonable, then ask your parent to listen to you while you explain your views. Offer him a better solution to the problem. Say, "I don't want to cancel all my plans for Saturday so you can take me to the furniture store for ten minutes and get my opinion on the sofa you've picked, but what if I go with you after field hockey practice tonight." If that approach doesn't work, then the problem may be that your parent needs to stay in a power struggle with you. All you can do at that point is keep clear in your own head about what makes sense and what doesn't, even if you have to give in to your parent's demand.

Another pattern in troubled families is that the parent gives in *too* easily. She never stands her ground with the child, even on important matters of safety or morality. The teen is left with more power than she really wants or is ready for and she's left with an absence of strong parental authority or guidance. The parent gives the message, "You've defeated me, exhausted me, bowled me over," which is scary because it means your parent isn't as strong as you'd like. Such weakness in a parent can also make the world seem like a sad and pointless place, because the adult who should have a strong sense that some things are worth standing and fighting for seems to have no such convictions.

Some parents give in easily not because they're overwhelmed but in order to manipulate another's feelings. They act as if you've overwhelmed them because they know you've got a sensitive nature, so you're likely to come back, apologize, and give in if you feel your parent has been saddened or offended. For example, you want to go to a party and your mom says no; she doesn't think the supervision will be good. You beg her to let you go and you promise her you'll be careful and keep safe. You continue explaining how responsible you'll be. "All right," your mother says wearily. She adds, "I just can't handle all the pressure you put me under. If I say no, you push and push until I get a migraine and I'm up all night in pain." You start to feel bad thinking about your mom's painful headache, so you tell her, "I won't go if you don't want me to. I'm sorry, Mom." "You do what you want," your mom says with a sigh. "My head hurts too much already for me to think straight."

Here, your mom has really manipulated you. If she believed the party was unsafe, she should have stuck to her guns and told you that you couldn't go. If she got tired of your making your case over and over, she could have told you she'd heard enough; her mind was made up. Instead, she gives in to your pleading and tells you her headache is your responsibility. You're left not knowing how she really feels about the party. The best thing you can do under the circumstances is to make your best judgment about whether the party is a safe situation or not, and act accordingly. You may also benefit from acknowledging some anger at your mom, who is letting you down by failing to maintain a concern about your safety.

Chapter 13

WHY PARENTS HAVE PROBLEMS

A little understanding of why your parent has the problems he does may help you. But first, let me give you a few words of caution. Number one: You won't be able to understand your parent's experience fully because you are young and your life experience has been very different from your parent's, so just aim at this point for a little understanding. More can come later. Number two: Understanding your parent won't make all your worries, anger, or disappointment melt away. It may help to an extent, but it won't eliminate those feelings. Understanding your parent actually may deepen certain painful feelings. Number three: Understanding your parent's emotional problems is not one of your basic responsibilities, in the way that school and social development are, so don't make it your job to understand your parent's difficulties in great depth. It's more appropriate for your parent and other adults to take on that job. If you feel that more knowledge will help you manage your situation, by all means seek that out, but don't feel it's your obligation to know all there is to know about your parent's problems.

I will look at a number of problems a parent may have and say just a little about each. The trouble-categories I'll cover are depression, anxiety, abuse, addiction, and psychosis. You can tell from the brevity of the list that more could be added.

DEPRESSION

Depression means that life feels very painful. Very little gives the depressed person pleasure. Many things distress him deeply. He is low on energy, enthusiasm, and hope for the future. He may be extremely irritable or he may be sad and obviously unhappy. He likely feels that life is of little worth and at times he might prefer death.

Some people get depressed because the chemical systems in their body and brain are out of whack. The majority of depressions result from people's efforts to flee painful or stressful emotions (or from some combination of out-of-whack feelings and out-of-whack chemicals). It may seem odd that people flee something painful by turning to something else that's painful, but that's exactly what happens. Depression—though it's painful—can seem like the best solution to an emotional problem. Here is an example of how a person might get depressed:

> When Brenda Jones was growing up, her father favored her older sister over her. Brenda found this painful and it angered her, but when she protested, her father said she was imagining things and she was too sensitive and overdramatic. She hated hearing those things because they left her feeling criticized and misunderstood, so she tried to keep her feelings of complaint to herself. It was hard carrying around bitter feelings, so after a while she started pretending to herself that everything was okay. She denied her bitter feelings about her father preferring her sister.

> When Brenda grew up and married Bob Jones, she felt she'd married a man who loved and respected her, but as she got a bit older and was not so attractive as she'd once been, her husband started to make disparaging comments about her appearance. He took to pointing out attractive women on the street and he nagged his wife to take aerobics classes and lose weight. The situation with her husband started to stir up anger in Brenda, since her husband was mistreating her. As she began to feel angry, something told her not to let the anger show. She didn't make a connection to her childhood experience with her father; she just "felt funny" about getting angry. She tried to stop her anger. She gave in to her husband's pressure and went to aerobics classes she didn't enjoy. She lost weight she didn't need to lose. She began to feel lifeless and more and more depressed.

Brenda's story shows how people can get depressed when they cut themselves off from their own feelings and wishes. Other roads may lead to depression. Some people get depressed because they feel the only way to have power in relation to others is to be sickly, which guarantees that people will give them attention and concern. Often, these people grew up in homes in which stating your needs directly brought ridicule, neglect, or hostility. But getting sick and sad brought some amount of sympathy and indulgence. They were rewarded for being sick and weak, not for being well and strong. Generally, depression results when a person feels helpless about getting legitimate needs met. The helplessness may be real—for example, when extreme poverty limits educational opportunity or when a death makes it impossible to experience the love of someone once near and dear. Or the helplessness may be a product of life experience that has cut a person off from some of her own emotional resources, for example, assertiveness, natural feelings of entitlement, and positive uses of anger. Brenda is an example of the second type of helplessness. She doesn't feel safe identifying her anger at her husband and using it to have a discussion with him about his changing attitude toward her.

ANXIETY

Like depression, anxiety is a painful state. Anxious people feel jittery and unable to relax. Sometimes, anxiety gets so strong that a person may feel she will pass out or have a heart attack and die. An anxious person's feelings won't settle down and her body won't relax either. She will want to retreat to a safe place, such as the home or bedroom. Sleeping becomes difficult, as may eating and working. Interacting with others may become very difficult. Some people are anxious much of the time. Others are generally relaxed but have "attacks" of anxiety periodically. For some people, the attacks are unpredictable. For others, they occur with a fairly clear pattern, for example, whenever the person goes to a crowded, public place such as a mall or supermarket.

As with depression, psychological factors and chemical factors both can contribute to anxiety. Some people seek relief by trying to understand their thoughts and feelings in psychotherapy, while others seek relief through medication or behavioral treatments. Doctors differ in which of these treatment approaches they recommend; some recommend a combination of approaches. Whenever possible, the doctor will want to know the cause of the anxiety. Anxiety caused by an overactive thyroid gland requires a treatment different from that appropriate to emotional conflicts.

When a person has complicated, conflicting wishes and fears, which she doesn't understand, anxiety often results. Say your mother gets extremely anxious whenever she is in a social situation. That situation might be a party or maybe a trip to your school to meet with your teachers. She tells herself there is nothing to fear in these situations, but she's terribly frightened nonetheless. She tells herself it's good to go to the party or the meeting and speak up and let people notice her and respond to her, but having those thoughts makes her heart race and she thinks she'll pass out or her mind will go blank.

If your mother went to a therapist to try to overcome her anxiety, she might discover that all through her childhood, her family gave her strong messages that children were not to call attention to themselves. If your mother's mother (your grandmother) saw a child who was happily twirling around and joking in front of adults, she would lecture your mother on how disgraceful that child's behavior was. She might even say that if any child of hers behaved like that she'd put the child up for adoption or give the child a well-deserved whipping. From time to time, your mother broke the family rules and called attention to herself in public. She was severely scolded, then given the silent treatment for days.

If you think about this life story, you may find it easier to understand how your mother fights with frightened feelings whenever she wants to go out into the world and do something that calls attention to her. She hasn't gotten over the lesson she learned as a young girl: calling attention to yourself brings humiliation and abandonment and means you are a bad and unlovable person.

I've given just one example of how anxiety develops. Other examples could be given. In many of them we would see a person in conflict over whether it's all right to keep hold of some behavior, thought, or feeling that's part of himself but has brought trouble with others, often when the person was very young. As people get older, the conflicts they have had with their parents often are taken inside the self. A conflict lives within the person, a conflict between a part of him that identifies with his parent's views and a part of him that speaks up for his own most basic needs and wishes. Of course, this kind of conflict only occurs when the parent's demands on the child were at odds with the child's natural self.

ABUSE

Abusing others can be a way to get rid of unwanted feelings about yourself or the life you've led. A man may feel powerless remembering the sexual abuse he suffered as a child. He may also feel extreme humiliation, hatred, and self-hatred. All these feelings darken his mood. He finds that when he kicks the dog or gets drunk and berates his son or hits his wife, he gets a feeling of power that counters the painful helplessness and self-contempt. This logic sounds very simple and in a way it is, but it leads to some complicated and destructive interactions between people.

If your mother comes from this kind of background and she mistreats you to try to settle her own distressed feelings, she'll be passing on to you the challenge she encountered and failed. That challenge is to understand the abuse you've suffered, to come to terms with it as well as you can, and to stop the cycle of abuse by treating others respectfully, not abusively.

Abusing others also can be a way to feel in control of rejections and disappointments. Say a person had many bad experiences of suddenly getting rejected, for no clear reason, just when he thought things were going well in a friendship. He gets to where he's afraid to relax and trust a relationship. He's afraid that things will blow up just when he's feeling comfortable. He discovers that if he provokes someone or mistreats her, she'll get angry and reject him. He likes that, in a funny sort of way, because the sequence of events is predictable. He knows exactly when the rejection will come. It will come when he *makes* it come. He sets the whole thing in motion himself. He no longer sits and waits helplessly for trouble.

If Mr. Washington is an abusive person who is, deep-down, afraid of rejection, his son, Gerald, may have the experience that just when he's feeling some closeness with his dad, his dad suddenly gets abusive. Gerald is totally confused. He doesn't know what on earth is going on. He doesn't understand that his father is afraid that the closeness between them will suddenly blow up, so his dad blows up the closeness himself.

ADDICTION

We have seen how getting depressed and abusing others can be ways to control feelings that are painful and seem overwhelming. Using alcohol or addictive drugs can serve a similar purpose. Drugs and alcohol bring immediate changes in how we feel. If we like the way the substances make us feel, we can take comfort in knowing that those substances can be used at will to wipe away pain. The substances give us power over things that otherwise make us feel powerless.

Unfortunately, using substances to wash away painful feelings takes a high toll. We may mistreat others or neglect them when using the substances, which leads to major problems in friendships or family life. A person's whole life becomes organized around seeking the escape the substances give him. He is less and less interested in day-to-day reality and less and less equipped to manage it, so he finds himself feeling weaker than ever, except when under the drug's influence. He becomes more and more convinced that the only good feelings he can have come from drugs, or with the help of drugs.

Some people use repetitive behaviors in the way others use drugs. An example would be gambling, or extramarital sexual affairs. For certain people, particular activities can be counted on to make them feel great. The activities wash away feelings of helplessness or frustration. The activities people use in this way aren't really so special or magical, but for certain people, they have a special meaning. If money is tremendously important to you and you think that you can make a huge amount of money from a small amount, through gambling, you may want desperately to gamble whenever you're feeling small or frustrated. If you think sexual "conquest" is the measure of a man's worth, you may have a powerful urge to seduce a woman when you feel belittled at work. Just as with drug or alcohol addictions, these behavior addictions give short-term relief and long-term headaches.

Addictive behaviors are defined not so much by the choice of behavior as by the way in which the behavior is used. Take exercise as an example. Your mother may love to swim because swimming makes her feel strong and attractive, and because she loves the feeling of moving through the water and the relaxation after her swim. There's nothing wrong with that; in fact, it's all very nice. But what if every time she has a conflict with you or an uncomfortable feeling about her body or her work life, instead of trying to think through and solve those problems, she instead rushes to the pool and while she strokes through the water, she blots out all her problems and worries? When she leaves the pool, she's forgotten her conflict with you and is less, not more ready to address it. And what if over time she gets to where she thinks about swimming for much of every day and if a day goes by and she can't swim, she's irritable and unreasonable with the people around her? Now swimming is operating as an addiction. It's become something used to avoid life, not something sought out because it's a pleasure. If it's your mother who is addicted to swimming, you will suffer as a consequence, since she will be preoccupied with swimming and will not be available emotionally to work out day-to-day problems and enjoy day-to-day pleasures with you. You may also suffer because her mood will go up and down depending on whether she can go swimming, in the same way that an alcoholic parent's mood may depend more on her alcohol use than on ordinary pleasures and frustrations.

PSYCHOSIS

The group of mental illnesses called psychoses includes schizophrenia, mania, and some of the more extreme depressions. A person who is psychotic doesn't see the world like most people do, at least some of the time. A paranoid schizophrenic person may believe the FBI is trying to kill her when they're not. A person suffering from mania may believe he is fabulously wealthy when he's not (and he may spend money as if it were a never-ending river). A person who has a psychotic depression may believe he is full of evil spirits and should be punished. He may try to punish himself by burning or cutting himself.

Living with a psychotic person is deeply frightening. Sometimes the person is suffering terribly and usually he is causing big problems for the people around him. You feel helpless to relieve the suffering or to stop the destructive behavior. That kind of helplessness can be highly stressful and painful.

Not everything about psychosis is understood. Some instances result from disorder in the brain caused by chemical abnormalities.

People can become temporarily psychotic from medications that disorganize their brains, or from extremely high fevers. Some people's brains seem to get chemically disturbed without their taking drugs or suffering from fevers. The disturbance may be a result of poor management of powerful emotional conflicts (for example, those stemming from early abuse or trauma), or it may result from an abnormality of the brain that is part of that individual's makeup.

Many people suffering from chemically-based psychoses can show some symptom relief if they take medications. Some people are greatly helped, though not all are. It's also the case that not all psychotic people like to take medications. Some don't like the way they feel on medications. Others feel frightened or suspicious of the medication. Paranoid people are often afraid of doctors and medications because they feel the treatment is a way to hurt or kill them.

It's almost impossible to reason with a person who is psychotic. You may see that what your mother is doing is terribly harmful to her and to others and you want to show her a better way of thinking about things, but she won't listen. It doesn't matter who tries to persuade her. You could be Einstein, the Pope or the President; you still wouldn't succeed.

Some psychoses are episodic, which means they come and go. For example, a person with a manic-depressive psychosis may have periods of time when he seems normal, periods of time when he is deeply depressed, and periods of time when he is manic. During a manic phase, the person may be on-the-go all the time, even in the middle of the night. He may also be high-spirited or, in some cases, short-tempered. Manic people are unreasonable. You can argue with them about their insistence on going to the movies at three o'clock in the morning, or about their spending $3000 on baseball cards, and they won't grasp your objection.

During a psychotic episode (which may be manic, depressive, or schizophrenic), a person may need to be in the hospital where he is protected from self-harm and from harming others. In the hospital, a person may be given medication and therapy, and basic needs such as food and shelter are met. Some people with psychotic illnesses make good, lasting recoveries, though usually that kind of progress takes a long time and a great amount of work. Others have lifelong illnesses that may be constant or may come and go.

Chapter 14

PROFESSIONAL HELP: WHEN AND HOW TO GET IT

How do you know when you or someone you know needs professional help? Three things are helpful to consider in looking at whether someone needs outside help. I'll call those things (a) Very Bad Situations, (b) Painful Feelings, and (c) Self-Defeating Behavior. Very Bad Situations can be helped by government agencies called Protective Services. Painful Feelings and Self-Defeating Behavior can often be helped by therapy from mental health professionals that includes specialists such as psychologists, social workers, psychoanalysts, and psychiatrists.

VERY BAD SITUATIONS

Any child who has a troubled parent has a bad situation with which to cope. That doesn't necessarily mean the child needs professional help, although lots of people in bad situations can make good use of professional help. However, certain extreme types of bad situations occur that *always* should be brought to the attention of professionals so that help can be provided; these I am calling Very Bad Situations. I am talking about instances in which a child is being sexually abused, physically abused, or the young person's basic needs (such as food, clothing, health care, shelter, and education) are being neglected. Some troubled parents are so *emotionally* abusive that a professional should be alerted just the same as if the parent were physically beating the child. By emotional abuse I mean things like battering a child with constant insults or holding a child responsible for major bad events that were not his doing (for example, the death of a brother or sister).

Abuse and neglect need to be brought to the attention of local agencies set up to protect kids. These agencies exist in all states, though they don't always go under the same name. For the moment, I'll call them all Protective Services. A young person can call Protective Services directly (for yourself or to report mistreatment of another child) or you can report abuse or neglect to professionals who are required by law to report to Protective Services. These professionals include people such as police, schoolteachers, physicians, school counselors, psychologists, psychiatrists, and social workers.

If a report is made to Protective Services, the agency worker will listen to what you describe and will decide whether the seriousness warrants an investigation. If the Protective Services worker feels that a child is being abused or seriously neglected at home, he or she will act to protect the child and to hold the adults accountable for their actions. If you are in doubt as to whether your situation or another child's should be reported to Protective Services, you should go ahead and report. If Protective Services' intervention isn't necessary, they will let you know. You can make a report to Protective Services without your parents being told who made the call. Even if your parents ask who made the report, that information can be kept secret.

If you want to locate the Protective Services agency in your community, you can get the name and number from your school, the police, or a local hospital. You can also look in the phonebook or on the Internet for an agency that deals with child abuse and neglect. Online, try searching 'Child Protection Services' and the name of your state. Or you can call the Department of Social Services, or the Department of Human Services for your state.

If you have reason to contact Protective Services, do what you need to in order to get the contact information you need. Remember, your schoolteacher, principal, or school nurse can help you, as can a doctor's office or community mental health clinic or police station. You can call those places and ask for the number for Protective Services without even giving your name. Protective services can also help older people who are being abused, so if you know of a situation like that–for example, an elderly person is being hit or underfed by a caretaker–you should report that situation to a trusted adult or to protective services.

PAINFUL FEELINGS

If you feel lousy from time to time, that's not so unusual and doesn't necessarily mean you should see a counselor or therapist. But if you feel lousy a lot of the time and the things you've tried on your own don't seem to be helping and others' advice hasn't helped much either, then it's time to think about consulting a therapist. If you've had strong wishes to hurt yourself or to hurt animals or other people, these too, are signs you should talk to a therapist. When it comes to seeing a therapist, it's always better to err on the safe side. If you go to a therapist once or twice and don't need to continue, no harm has been done. And you'll have someone you can call if you ever need to talk in the future. On the other hand, if you're in pain or in trouble and you are too afraid to get help, you may do yourself some real harm by not getting what you need.

SELF-DEFEATING BEHAVIORS

Self-defeating behavior means you keep on doing things that are no good for you. You get in your own way; you are your own worst enemy. If you keep on doing things that lead to failure and your efforts to stop tripping yourself up don't work out and you're stumped about why you keep yourself from succeeding, those are good reasons to talk to a therapist who may be able to help you understand and put a stop to your self-defeating behavior. Examples of self-defeating behavior are failing in school or sports even though you are capable of success, alienating your friends over and over, having sex with people who don't really care about you, setting yourself up for punishment and unhappiness by driving drunk, revealing dangerously personal things on Facebook, or making friends with irresponsible or abusive people.

THERAPY AND THERAPISTS

Here's a story that gives you a reasonable way to think about therapy. Say you're a farmer and you're trying to get your crop of beans to the market. You've got so many beans that you have to make many trips carrying bags and bags of beans. You've walked back and forth to the market all day long and you're getting pretty tired and only a small fraction of your crop has made it to market. A friend comes along and says, "You can borrow my horse and wagon to get your beans to market more quickly. If you can tell me what market you're trying to get to, I'll go along with you and help you steer the wagon." What would a sensible person do? You'd use the horse and wagon, right? A therapist is someone who helps you get where you want to go when you're having trouble getting there on your own.

Okay, you may say, so I need some help. But what exactly is therapy? How will it help me get my beans to market faster? What actually happens if I go see a therapist? Therapy can help you understand some complicated things about how people work, but the basic activity is simple. You just sit in a chair and talk to the therapist about whatever you're thinking about or feeling or what you've been doing lately or what interests you in life. The therapist, on his or her part, listens attentively to what you say and tries to use what you share about yourself as a road to understanding where you may be getting hung up in meeting some of your goals. If you find it hard to talk about yourself and you get stuck, the therapist will try to help you get unstuck.

Here's an example of something that could happen in psychotherapy. Say you're talking about school and about how you keep failing tests even when you know the material, and you and Dr. Smith are puzzling about why that might be. Maybe later in the hour you describe a few times when you did very well in school or sports. Then you start talking about your dad's job failures and how depressed he's been lately. When he watches TV and stories are aired about people who are big successes, he can't bear to watch. He turns off the show. Sometimes you worry he'll commit suicide.

Listening to you, Dr. Smith might start to wonder whether you're afraid your success might further depress your dad. You might even be starting to wonder about that yourself, without Dr. Smith saying a word, because in talking out loud about your life you noticed for the first time how much you feel your dad is troubled by other people's successes. It may help you quite a bit to realize that you've been holding yourself back in school out of concern for your dad. You'll be able to think about whether it's really a good idea for you to defeat yourself in that way. You can think about whether in the long run your failure actually is helping your dad.

The kind of therapy you and Dr. Smith are doing is called Psychodynamic Psychotherapy because it focuses on the dynamics of your psyche, or mind. In other words, it focuses on what makes you tick, what makes your mind work the way it does. People often find this work very interesting and they enjoy having someone who is listening attentively and interested in how their mind and emotions work. Other varieties of therapy exist. Individuals may vary in what type of therapy works best for them. One type of therapy is called Cognitive Behavioral Therapy, or CBT. CBT is more structured than Psychodynamic Psychotherapy and may involve exercises the therapist will give the client to help her practice new skills. The core of CBT is the relationship among a person's thoughts, behaviors, and feelings. The therapist will help the person look closely at her thoughts and behaviors in order to pick out self-defeating patterns she may want to alter. All therapies depend in part on a good relationship developing between the therapist and the person seeking help.

Sometimes kids think of therapy as something young people get roped into, something that's forced on them because parents want to control them or want them to think they're crazy. That's an unfortunate way to approach therapy. If you walk in the door with that attitude, you won't allow the therapist to be your helper. The best way to go to therapy is out of choice, because you've decided you want some help. You don't wait until things fall apart totally and someone has to twist your arm into going.

If you did wait too long and your life *has* fallen apart badly and someone is pressuring you to go to therapy, you can still go with an attitude that lets you get help. You don't have to kick and scream and pretend something awful is being forced on you. If you're feeling forced into therapy, it may be helpful to step back and think about whether the direction you're being pushed and the direction you'd like to walk might be one and the same. If so, walk!

If you are a teenager, you may be reluctant to go to a professional because professionals are adults and you are at the age where you may be wanting to move away from adults, not get closer. A good therapist isn't going to interfere with your becoming independent. She'll try to help you to grow toward independence successfully.

Some kids fear that the therapist will be an extension of their parent. That's particularly scary if your parent is a troubled person who is highly critical of you, has no faith in you or wants you to give up teenage activities and act like a young child. A good therapist will be there to work *for you,* not to do your parent's bidding. The therapist may meet with your parent, but she'll be keeping your needs and your feelings and ideas in mind. Sometimes the therapist may challenge you to do better or she may confront you if you're being dishonest or screwing up, but she should be doing that to help you grow up in a healthy way, not because your parent directed her to.

I've been making comments about therapies where just you and a therapist meet, but a therapist also may recommend approaches such as family therapy, parent guidance or some combination of therapies. Whether a therapist sees an individual or the whole family depends in part on how that therapist works and in part on what's wrong in the family. It also depends on who in the family is willing to make an effort to improve things. Sometimes only the healthiest family member goes into therapy. The members with the biggest problems refuse therapy. That might seem odd or backward, but it's often the healthiest people who are most able to work hard to improve their lives. Sometimes kids of troubled parents complain, "My mom should be in therapy, not me." That's an understandable complaint, but therapy works best for those who want to make use of it and your mom may not be willing even though you are. So even though your mom may be more trou- bled than you, you may want to take the opportunity to get therapy in order to help yourself grow up to be healthy. Therapy really is a spe- cial opportunity, not one that everyone gets. Try to think of it as a gift to you, not a punishment or condemnation.

PARENT GUIDANCE

Parent guidance is professional help a parent can get to assist her or him in being a better parent. Some parents realize they're having difficulty parenting and will go on their own for help. Some parents respond well to a child or an adult friend or relative suggesting they get help parenting. The suggestion makes the parent recognize a prob- lem she's been slow to see on her own. Other parents are very op - posed to getting help and will get angry or feel dejected if anyone has the good sense to suggest parent guidance.

If you feel your parent needs help parenting, you can suggest parent guidance or therapy. If he refuses to get help, or if you feel there's no point in even suggesting it because you're certain your parent won't listen, you might benefit from talking to a therapist yourself. The therapist may be able to help you cope with the bad parenting you're getting.

FAMILY THERAPY

If a whole family goes into therapy, the therapist takes note of how the family members interact. The therapist points out destructive behaviors and tries to bring to light important things about which the family isn't communicating. The therapist's suggestions and observations and the new experiences the family has while interacting during therapy all give the family a chance to become a better functioning unit.

If you'd like to talk with a therapist or you think your family or parents should, you will need some help finding someone well qualified and you will need some help working out arrangements such as finances and transportation. If you have a parent you can talk with about the idea of seeing a therapist, go ahead and talk to your parent: that's the easiest route. Another route is to talk first to your school counselor, or even to a trusted schoolteacher or another adult who might give you some direction or perhaps help you approach your parent. A third possibility is to call a local agency such as Catholic Social Services, Community Mental Health or Jewish Child and Family Services. Even if your family has no money for therapy, help may be available. Sometimes insurance pays for therapy, or therapy may be provided at very low cost to those without the ability to pay. Schools often provide free counseling and can help with referrals to therapists in the community if more help is needed.

GETTING HELP FOR A FRIEND OR SIBLING

If you have a friend, sibling, or classmate who needs help, it's a kind and responsible act to try to assist that person in getting that help. A word of caution though, remember your limits. You can suggest to a friend that he or she get help, or talk to an adult who cares about children, but you can't force a person to get help or to stop self-destructive behavior. Also keep in mind that if you do step in, your friend may not meet you with gratitude. Your friend or sister or cousin may get angry with you instead of thanking you. The anger comes out of fear, so try not to let it bother you too much. Just keep focused on trying to do what your best judgment tells you is right. If the person gets help, down the road he'll be very glad you spoke up.

If you hear someone talking about an extreme behavior such as suicide or committing a harmful act against another, definitely report what you've heard to a trusted adult. The harmful act might be something criminal such as a shooting, rape, or use of an illegal drug, or something likely to cause emotional damage, such as posting a compromising photo of a peer on the Internet.

Chapter 15

FINISHING UP

First, congratulations on taking a journey by reading this book. Before finishing, it will be good to review some of the main ideas we've covered.

One of the ideas I think is important is that every person needs to use his or her own brain and mind to think about what's happening in his or her life. That might sound obvious, but kids who live with troubled parents often are pressured not to use their intelligence to make sense of the world around them. But just as you keep your eyes and ears open and active when you make your way in the world, you need to use your intelligence. Your own ideas can be a very important guide. You wouldn't let someone tell you red is blue, or a horse is a frog, so don't let anyone tell you what's wrong is right, what's mean is nice, what's hurtful is pleasurable, or anything else that's scrambled and nonsensical.

Using your head isn't the same thing as being pig-headed. It doesn't mean closing your mind to other people's ideas. It means that you filter the ideas other people give you through your own mind so that you know which ideas you want to take in and value, and which ideas make no sense to you. When you reject ideas, you can reject them absolutely and for all time if you're certain they're unsound. Or, if you're less sure, you can say, that makes no sense to me now, but the person who offered it is smart and well-intentioned so I'll keep the idea in mind, in case I want to rethink it later.

Another main point of this book is that being a parent doesn't automatically make a person wise, fair, responsible or any other good thing. That's unfortunate. It would be nice if all parents had those fine traits. But that's not the way things actually work. In reality, some parents are generally quite thoughtful, even-handed and reliable. And some parents are quite unwise, unfair and irresponsible. And many are in between.

Now we should go back to the first point (the one about using your head), and say, it's important to know whether your parent is acting with wisdom and fairness and acting responsibly, or whether he's not. Using your head can help you make those judgments. You're absolutely entitled to make them; you needn't feel guilty or disloyal for doing so. Remember, if your parent comes up short, that's not your doing. You're *seeing* it, not creating it. (If *you* come up short, you can take responsibility for that and try to change.)

If you have a parent (or two) who falls short in his or her parenting, you've had some bad luck. There's no reason other than bad luck for your having a sick, mean, or alcoholic parent. It's not because you're a bad person or an undeserving person. I don't think it's because God is giving you a special challenge either. Some people might not agree with me on that, but that's my view. You've just had some bad luck; that's all there is to it.

Having one piece of bad luck, even a big one, doesn't mean you're forever and in all ways an unlucky person. It doesn't mean you'll get sick and die young, or marry an awful person, or lose all your money. You may win the lottery, or the Nobel Prize (though that wouldn't be by luck!). You may become a Senator or a fine scientist or musician. So try to keep in mind that this one bad-luck thing in your life doesn't make you any certain kind of person. And it doesn't mean you're going to have a bad life.

In dealing with a troubled parent and a troubling home life, it's important to face the reality that's there. If you get too involved in pretending things aren't the way they are (for example, you refuse to believe your dad's an alcoholic when he is), or if you go off in a fantasy world and get every one of your pleasures in faraway, private places, you'll handicap yourself in the future. You'll get too invested in keeping your eyes closed and blocking things out, which takes a lot of energy that could be better spent on other things. Or you'll get too attached to your fantasy world and not put any effort into the day-to-day world that involves other people and shared activities.

The more you can face the realities of your home situation, the more you can adjust in healthy ways. Often that means turning to people outside your home for your pleasures and support, or to your healthier parent if you have one. One of the big mistakes kids with troubled parents can make is the mistake of believing that all people are as unreliable, mean, or sickly as one disappointing parent may be. Try hard to keep your eyes open so you can see the people around you as they are, which means seeing shortcomings and also strengths.

I've already said that your future doesn't need to be like your past. If your past has been unhappy, your future can be better. That's more likely to happen if you are active in trying to improve the things you don't like. Certain things you can't improve because they're not under your control. Your parent's behavior and feelings are examples of things you can't change. But your own behavior and feelings *can* be changed over time. Of course, making those changes isn't simple, but I hope this book has given you some ideas about how to get on the right road. And don't hesitate to ask for help when you're traveling down that road. Smart, strong people often do just that.

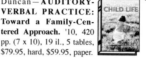